AIR TRAFFIC CONTROL

ALL'S NOT CLEAR OUT THE TOWER WINDOW

ROY T CUSHWAY

 **FriesenPress**

Suite 300 - 990 Fort St
Victoria, BC, Canada, V8V 3K2
www.friesenpress.com

ISBN
978-1-4602-5988-7 (Paperback)
978-1-4602-5989-4 (eBook)

1. Biography & Autobiography, Law Enforcement

Distributed to the trade by The Ingram Book Company

TABLE OF CONTENTS

"Thank you to my wife, Judy Lang Cushway and daughter, Dorothy Cushway for the help you have given me in getting this book published from my old original computer, emails and paper copies as well as all the re-typing and editing in order for me to publish a memoir of my years as an Air Traffic Controller"

Roy Cushway

Roy Cushway

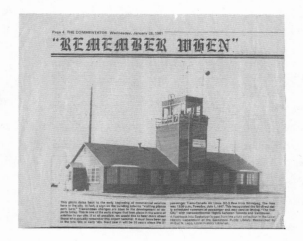

First Sask Control Tower

First Air Traffic Controller

Winnipeg Tower 1940 – 1962

First Control Tower Cleveland OH U.S.A.

First U.S.A Control Centre

10 COMMANDMENTS FOR PILOTS

1. Seat thyself well upon thy fifth vertebra-leaving not thy finger-prints on the controls and chewing not thy fingernails.

2. Know thy instruments; for they are the true and appointed profits.

3. Follow the indications of thy instruments; and verily the airplane will follow along, even as follows the tail of the sheep.

4. Do not stick out thy neck a foot stay within the confines of thy ability, and thou shalt live to a happy old age.

5. Know the appointed words and approved methods; so that if thy neck drapeth out, thou shalt be able even unto thyself to place same in its proper place, upon thy shoulders.

6. Follow thy radio beam; for their ways are happy ways and will lead to the promised landing.

7. Listen carefully; Yea verily, to the signal impinging on thy eardrum, for sometimes they seem to have the tongues of snakes, and will cross thy orientation, to the sad state where thou must have Heaven Herself for guidance.

8. Assume not, neither shalt thou guess; that thy position is such but prove to thine own satisfaction that such is the case.

9. Boast not, neither brag; for surely Old Devil Overcast shall write such words in his book, and thou shalt, some day, be called for an accounting.

10. Trust not thy seat(of thy pants),but follow thy instruments, read and truly interpret the word as given from thy instruments board, know that responsibility lies not with the hand that rocks the control column, but in and with the mind that directs the hand, and thou shalt be blessed with a long and happy life.

TO ALL OLD CONTROLLERS

A Man Knocked at The
Heavenly Gate
His Face Was Scarred
and Old ....
He Stood Before The
Man of Fate
For Admission To The
Fold........
" What Have You Done,"
St. Peter asked,
"To Gain Admission Here ? "

"I Have Been a Controller, Sir,
For Many and Many a Year."
The Pearly Gates Swung
Open Wide,.........

St. Peter Touched the Bell,
" Come In and Choose your
Harp", He said,
"You've Had Your Share of
HELL."

AIR
TRAFFIC
CONTROL

ALL'S NOT
CLEAR OUT THE
TOWER WINDOW

ROY T CUSHWAY

Air Traffic Control
- Book 1

Getting started on this book seems to be the hardest part of the exercise. After the material has been organized, and some idea of where to start is determined, then I find myself sitting in front of the typewriter trying to decide what to say. My thoughts are all over the place, and so, have decided to write whatever comes to mind and not to worry about the exact order of events, so long as they occur somewhere near the beginning of this story. So here I go.

Air Traffic Control was not in any of my plans when I was in High School at Central Collegiate in Moose Jaw, Saskatchewan. It is strange how a persons' life is changed from time to time due to circumstances beyond one's control. Sometimes it goes the wrong way and then sometimes it goes the right way; at least it seems so in your favor.

My Family

My only sister, Dorothy, died in 1932 at age 18 of meningitis. My oldest brother Lenny, sometimes called Swede because of his black hair, was killed in an industrial accident in 1942. My father who was a car-man for the CPR had contracted TB and was in Fort Qu'Appelle Sanatorium, where they collapsed one of his lungs. My second oldest brother, Al, was married and gone from home. Another brother, Doug, four years older than I, had joined the army and was somewhere overseas.

There was no one but my Mother and myself at home, and we were on relief, which is known nowadays as welfare, so as I was just finishing grade 11 in 1943, I decided to leave school, and go to work to try to improve our standard of living, and not have to live on handouts from others. My Dad finally came home much later, but continued to smoke, his heart weakened and he died in 1949 in Moose Jaw.

In the fall of 1943 I started working for Swift Canadian Company as an office boy, bringing home $15 per week. About a year later, I felt working in the plant would give me more experience and more pay than the office boy. Over the next four years I gained a great deal of experience working in every department from cold storage to shipping clerk. The pay was 75 cents per hour which was Top Wage for labor at that time. At home our living standard was raised slightly, plus we enjoyed all the choice cuts of meat at packing plant prices. Roast beef, lamb chops, sweetbreads, tenderloins were all affordable and available.

My position at the plant had been frozen and when I received my call up for duty in the Army; it was rejected by Swifts. That sequence of events probably was considered a gift from God because my mother had had more than her share of tragedy up to that point in time. In 1944 we received a telegram that my brother, Doug, had been injured by a land mine somewhere in Florence, Italy. He had both legs blown off and was not expected to live.

For four years from 1946 I was in business for myself operating a soft drink franchise which involved long hours from 6 am to midnight, 7 days a week. I lived at home until 1948, and then I moved to Regina to open up a new territory in the City and the country. During this time, Jack McGrath, my railway mail clerk friend and I, decided to go to Mexico City by train. (That's another story) This was to be my last fling before marrying Jean, the lady I had been courting for 10 years.

They made a Seaman out of me

In January, 1951, the Naval Reserves of which I was a member had an opening for one seaman for a month on a frigate, HMCS Antigonish, from Victoria, B.C. to Acapulco, Mexico. After discussing this with my fiancé, Jean, we postponed our wedding until April so that I could go.

I worked part ship with other seamen on the forecastle. The naval communications was split into two groups, CW operators and Visual operators. I chose visual because we had the privilege of working in the radio shack. When radio silence was invoked we worked the Aldis lamp. I also had the pleasant job of running up those pretty flags to the yardarm.

On return to Regina, it was time to settle down, so Jean and I got married and moved to an apartment. I decided that a career as a radio operator with Department of Transport, or similar company would be an interesting way to go. I needed time to study so I quit my soft drink business, and hired on as a Trolley Bus Operator for the City of Regina. I worked spare board for two years which gave me ample time to study.

How it all started

In the summer of 1954, I spotted a poster in the Post Office advertising for an Air Traffic Control Assistant. The closing date was July 27th. After talking it over with Jean, and visiting the local Tower in Regina, I decided it was related to communications and I would enjoy that. So I was excited to apply,

The Poster Read:
Department of Transport - Winnipeg Air Services District

Open to qualified residents of the Winnipeg Air Services District, which consists of the Provinces of Manitoba, Saskatchewan,

Western Ontario as far East as the 88th Meridian and the Northwest Territories lying to the North.

It is proposed to establish an eligible list as a result of this competition, from which vacancies at Winnipeg, Man. and Saskatoon, Sask. will be filled as they occur.

AIR TRAFFIC CONTROL ASSISTANT
Salary - $2,370 - $3,120 per year

Duties: Under direction, to assist the Air Traffic Controller on duty as required, in the control of air traffic; to receive, relay and transmit messages by telephone, teletype or radiotelephone: to maintain a chronological record of all aircraft arrivals and departures; to operate air traffic control equipment; and to perform other related duties as required.

Desirable qualifications: Some high school education; satisfactory physical condition as required by Canadian Air Regulations for Air Traffic Controllers; good enunciation; personal suitability. Additional credits will be given for related experience.

Other Information:

1. The Air Traffic Control Service is, in general, on a twenty-four hour day, seven-day week basis. Air Traffic Control Assistants are required to work on rotating shifts.

2. A probationary period is provided for training purposes during which appointees will be required to obtain a certificate as an Air Traffic Controller. Trainees who do not obtain a certificate within the designated period may be released.

3. Vacant positions for Air Traffic Controller, Grade 1 throughout Western Canada are filled by promotion from among the Certificated Assistants. Air Traffic Controllers, Grade 1 are eligible for promotion to the higher grades in the service. Certificated Air Traffic Control Assistants employed in

Traffic Control Tower may be required to control traffic without the direct supervision of an Air Traffic Controller, if circumstances so necessitate.

Important: Prior to reporting for duty each successful candidate will be required t produce, at own expense, a medical certificate on the prescribed form.

Age Limit: The Department of Transport is not prepared to accept for appointment any candidates who have reached their thirtieth birthday on the closing date for receipt of applications.

Where to apply: Application forms are available at the nearest Office of the Civil Service Commission, Post Office, or National Employment Office. All applicants (veteran and non-veteran) should apply to the Civil Service Commission, 356 Main St., Winnipeg, Manitoba, NOT LATER THAN JULY 27, 1954.

COMPETITION NUMBER - 54-W3612- SHOULD BE QUOTED.
OTTAWA, JULY 6, 1954

The wording on this poster was quite different than the competition posters that were distributed at later dates.

The salary, for one thing, is a good example, albeit in 1954, $2,370 per annum was a respectable one, it no way compared to the starting salary in 1986 of $13,000. The system then, and the workload of the controller, will be compared to 1986, to find the reason for the change in salaries and entry qualifications.

Waiting

When I applied for the Air Traffic Control Assistant in May 1954, I didn't know of the slowness of the bureaucracy, and could have saved myself many hours waiting for the mailman. On June 8, 1954, I received the long awaited letter stating that I had been placed on the eligible list. I hurried off to the Medical Officer to have the required medical, and to get the show on the road.

The **All Important** letter arrived at the end of June requesting me to appear before a selection board in Regina. The Board members were - Claude Brereton, Nels Harvey and a local Civil Service Personnel Office. Claude was Chief of the Winnipeg Centre, and Nels was Chief of the Winnipeg Tower. I was accepted and found out that I would be training and working under the watchful eyes of these two fine gentlemen. In August, 1954, Jean and I moved from a water drenched basement suite to an apartment in downtown Winnipeg. This was the beginning of my 30 year career as an Air Traffic Controller.

WINNIPEG CENTRE - WINNIPEG TOWER
The old Control Centre - How it was.....

In 1954 two very important events took place in the field of aviation.

The U-2 Aircraft was born; the brainchild of a thirty-nine year old engineering prodigy named Trevor Gardner. This aircraft was built in less than eight months, and in the air flying at altitudes above 70,000 feet for periods of 10 - 12 hours without refueling. It was later called the "Black Lady of Espionage" by Francis Gary Power, 1956.

The other event took place at 10:00 a.m. on a bright sunny day in Moose Jaw, Saskatchewan. A NATO student, flying a Harvard aircraft had just taken off from the airbase south of the city and was cleaning up his aircraft at 4000 feet VFR (Visual Flight Rules) over the Exhibition grounds on the north side of the city, on a heading of 360 degrees. A Trans-Canada Airlines, Northstar was westbound, also at 4,000 feet IFR (Instrument Flight Rules) in VFR conditions when the Harvard slammed into the left underside of the airliner killing all passengers and crew of both aircraft. That was the worst accident in airline history in Canada, April 8, 1954 - 37 were killed, 31 passengers, 4 crew, and 2 air force pilots. The rules and procedures of Air Traffic Control changed dramatically, with the rapid growth of Civil and Military training, increased speed and altitude.

When I arrived at Winnipeg Centre to begin my formal training I was given a tour of the Centre where I was to be working. This did not take too long as the Controllers on duty were very busy. The size of the workspace was smaller than most living rooms At 14 x 20. The four Controllers and the Chief of the Unit were controlling all aircraft flying IFR from the Lakehead west to the Alberta border. There was a large sign above the Winnipeg control position that pretty well summed up the situation as far as the Controllers were concerned.

"IF YOU CAN KEEP YOUR HEAD WHEN ALL ABOUT YOU ARE LOSING THEIRS, THEN YOU JUST DON'T UNDERSTAND THE SITUATION"

The other facility, where I was to be training was the Winnipeg Tower. This work place was slightly larger than our bathroom and looked like an abandoned steel tower with a glass enclosure on the top.

Inside Controllers were speaking a language I didn't understand, and the Pilot's responses were unintelligible to my ears!

After my indoctrination to the work area, and introductions, I was assigned to train with one of the B stands. There were two B stands on duty to assist the Controllers with message handling, weather information and many more tasks that occur during a tour of duty. We were told that when the Controllers said "Jump", we should respond "How High?" I was to keep out of the way as much as possible, but to stay within earshot when we were needed. It was easy to understand why.

Because of the small workspace, the noise level increased as the traffic built up each day. There were four Controllers on duty, and their workload was extraordinarily heavy. They grumbled now and then, but they were glad to be doing the job they did because of the challenge, plus the feeling they were performing a very necessary service to all concerned. One of the Controllers would sit back in his chair during a lull in air traffic, close his eyes, and dream of the Peach Orchard that he hoped to have someday in the Okanagan Valley of British Columbia.

In the stories throughout the book I will use real names whenever I can remember them. (That's the first of three things that happen upon retirement; I can't remember the other two, so some fictitious names will be used to protect the innocent.)

When a new Controller is assigned to a unit, one of the first things he gets with his indoctrination is a set of initials. Usually his own Initials will be used, except, as in my case someone already used those initials. My initials are RTC, but Richard Cowan was using RC; Robert Turner was RT and Torchy Cowan was TC, so I adopted TR. These initials are used with all transmissions when using landlines. All conversations are recorded so that if there are enquiries or procedures to be checked, all persons are easily identified. The initials remained with each Controller throughout his career and quite often ATC personnel call each other by their operating initials. Although I am now retired I have my ATC initials as part of my Personal e-mail address (tratc25@gmail.com).

All the Controllers except two or three, in the Winnipeg Centre were Veterans. Vic Skinner (VS) had been a fighter pilot who lost a leg during the war. He smoked a pipe, and even when there was no tobacco in the pipe bowl he would chew on it. His bottom teeth were worn down to gum level. He had scrounged an old passenger seat from a DC3 Aircraft that he would use when he was relaxing between busy periods. Vic was an excellent controller and eventually became Chief of the Centre. He has now gone to that Control Centre in the Sky, where so many controller friends and colleagues have joined him.

All the Controllers in this business were excellent; each one had an individual way of doing the same thing. Rolly Porter (RP) was the smallest one there at that time, but he had a strong voice and everyone knew when he was around. Dudley Dorsett (DD) had long black hair in pompadour style, heavy eyebrows, wore glasses, smoked cigars and a pipe. George G. Smith (GG) was soft spoken, smoked a pipe, and would tell you exactly how a grapefruit should be cut and eaten. Bill Kelloch (WK) was short, slightly stout, wore glasses, didn't smoke, and was not a veteran which I think the other Controllers gave him a hard time about. He would volunteer to work most of the midnight shifts just so that he could avoid the bugging and unpleasant atmosphere during the day shifts. Ray Peden (PR) was tall and slim, bespectacled with a very quiet manner, except at a staff Christmas party for tower and centre personnel at Jack's Place, south of Winnipeg. There was a lull in the music from the orchestra, so everyone went back to their seats, or to the bar, or food buffet. Ray was standing in the middle of the floor with a pickle in his hand, waving it around, as though he was scolding, or trying to get a point across to the Tower Chief. He hadn't noticed the music had stopped, and that he was alone in the middle of the floor. Everyone had a laugh about that. Robert Turner (RT) was a blond, suave, debonair, quiet controller. He was the guy dreaming about the peach orchard. I think he used that as an escape from the pressure of the rat race in the Centre. Bob had another favorite expression when things got hot and heavy.

"ONE OF THESE DAYS THE WHOLE THING IS GOING TO BLOW UP"

The Control Centre was small and the smell of smoke was heavy at times but you had to tolerate it then. Everyone brown-bagged lunch, because there was nowhere close to eat out. The control board was set up with four sectors: Winnipeg (about 30 mile radius of the Airport); Winnipeg West included Portage and MacDonald Airports (RCAF) to Yorkton, Sask. Regina, Moose Jaw and Saskatoon airports sector; Winnipeg East - including Gimli (RCAF), and Lakehead airport (Now Thunder bay).

The Controller's aids were primitive by today's standards, but as air traffic increased so did the facilities and the Controller's aids, but they always seemed to be one or two steps behind. All the rules and regulations for Controllers were contained in one small book.

These of course had to change with progress and today they involve a manual about two inches thick covering two volumes of procedures, and many more covering rules, notams, equipment, administration, directives, etc.

All the controlling in the Centre was done by a telephone system to other Radio Operators and Tower Controllers. The Winnipeg Controller had one frequency to talk directly to aircraft inbound or outbound or to and from Winnipeg. The switchboard system on the control panel was duplicated on two desks at the rear, for the B stand. Every day was a busy day in the centre and the noise level was nerve wracking. Phones ringing, bells ringing, and voices rose to get a message across. There was no stopping for meal breaks; eating on the job was the way of life for Controllers.

EMBRYONIC TRAFFIC AND TYPES OF AIRCRAFT

In 1954 - 55, the jet age was beginning, so the rules of the air began to change rapidly over the next several years. As a matter of fact they are constantly changing and continue to do so. The T-33 was the Military trainer at this time, and there were many stationed in Gimli, Portage and MacDonald bases in Manitoba. Of course the other old reliable workhorses were still prevalent here and scattered across Canada. Harvard's, B25's, C45's, Cessna, Argus, DC3's, Helicopters, C119's, F86's, CF 100's, CF 101's, North stars, and Britannia's. Trans Canada Airlines were flying North Stars, DC3's, Super Connie & the Bristol Freighter. The first time I gave landing instructions to a Bristol coming in to land on Runway 36 from the north, I blew it. We were programmed to say "Check wheels down and locked", after giving landing instructions. The Bristol Freighter had fixed under carriage. The

Pilot was quick to respond with "down and welded". One thousand on top was a new term being used to accommodate a lot of aircraft in the sky at the same time.

The meaning of the term was basically that an aircraft could go up above the cloud at least 1,000 feet, and fly by the Visual Flight Rules (VFR). A clearance was needed to get above the cloud, and again when the aircraft decided to come out of the cloud. The Jet aircraft would generally go above 20,000 feet, and the piston planes would fly at the lower levels, sometimes between the cloud layers.

Civilian aircraft were able to live with this arrangement because they were all piston, and flying at lower levels. There were problems from time to time but the system was still safe. The Department of Transport did not have Radar. There was an American Early Warning Radar site just east of Winnipeg at Milner Ridge, which was available for emergencies. The main nav-aids were Radio Ranges, some beacons and few stations had Automatic Direction Finders (ADF)

Mayday, Mayday, Mayday

NATO training was increasing and the skies would fill up with students and instructors from the three RCAF bases in Manitoba. Winnipeg had a large RCAF training station based on the west side of Stevenson Airport (Winnipeg International Airport). During my first week at the new job, I heard a Mayday call on 121.5 Mhz. from a T-33 lost on a navigation trip. The Radio Station was in the next room to the Centre and when the radio volume was turned up we could hear everything from where we were sitting. I was involved in a lot of emergencies during my career, but this was the only time I heard the words "Mayday, Mayday, Mayday" being used to signal that such an event was taking place. The pilot talked in calm and collected voice as the ground stations were frantically trying to get a fix on the aircraft. Finally the pilot said, he was out of fuel, the engines had stopped running, and he said "I'm going to leave her now". Then there was silence.

The T-33 crashed near a graveyard south of the Manitoba border. The pilot parachuted safely into a farmer's field.

Friendships grew rapidly at the Winnipeg Centre. The Tower Controllers and the Centre Controllers were a close-knit group. The profession was unknown by the average person on the street. Whenever someone asked where I worked, that was confirmed. When I replied I worked for the Department of Transport, it was assumed I worked in one of three areas: 1. Truck Driver; 2. Royal Canadian Air Force or; 3. Trans Canada Airlines. Controllers pretty well stuck together as a group, mainly because no one understood our language. The thing uppermost on our minds was to replay last week's or today's problems and to talk about them with someone who understood us.

Most pilots were friendly and understood that most problems were due to the system, and not to the Controllers. To err is human and this can happen to a Controller or Pilot anytime. When I was taking my training in the Winnipeg Tower my guiding light was Hank Batt, who is now in that Control Tower in the Sky. Hank made it very clear to me from the start that I was to make my own decisions, make them right, and stick to them.

Don't let someone senior change your mind because, he said, if you make a mistake, and you turn around to see where everyone is, there will be no one there. Even your best friend won't know you. You will be left holding the mic all alone. This advice proved to be some of the best I got throughout my career. I saw it happen to other Controllers many times.

The Winnipeg Tower was just that, a Tower. It was a steel tower with a glass box on top, about 70 feet high with a zigzag staircase on the outside. The Winnipeg Flying Club was built along the north side of the Tower. There was no lunchroom, bathroom, or reading room. The heat was supplied by old electric floor heaters, originally used in railway cars and converted to 120V. We used to toast our sandwiches on them. A water jug stood in the corner, like you see in offices, with everyone congregated around it. On cold winter nights it was a long way to the bathroom, so some of the guys would just relieve themselves over the railing. The Flying Club manager asked us not to do this, as when it was freezing, with a south wind blowing, it would freeze to their lounge windows, and no one could see out!!

Bring on the ladies

There were very few women in ATC at that time; one in Edmonton, one in Montreal, and Beth Russell in Winnipeg. Beth was an excellent controller and she was well liked by everyone in the business. I admired her very much and she taught me a few lessons, although I was never assigned as a trainee to her.

There was a girl hired shortly after me. Marg Quinn became a good controller, but because women were a minority and new to the profession, some of the guys gave them a hard time. I think that quite often, Beth would try to give me a bad time when I was working on her shift, just because of that. Torchy Cowan came on the scene about this time. He was an ex-air force type who still flew Mustangs for the Reserve. He was called a Weekend Warrior. He and Marg struck a note with each other, soon married and moved to Regina where Torchy signed on as an airline Pilot with CPA, and Marg continued as a controller for a short time.

Jack Dodd was an old aberrant seasoned Controller with very little hair. They say he pulled it all out trying to control the Weekend Warriors. Usually there would be four or five of them up in the air at the same time and they would either spring an oil leak, or the gear would stick half up, or they would come screaming into the circuit at 200 knots and disrupt poor Jack's neat and orderly circuit patterns. The Tower Controllers' mic hung from the ceiling on a long curly cord so that Controllers had some mobility to see out the backside of the tower. Jack would be stomping around, hollering into the mic, and when it was all over he would get on the phone, and do it all again. Jack was also a Reservist so he swung a bit of weight over at the other side with the Reserve Squadron.

The procedures for a new trainee to follow were quite simple. Do all of the work of the B stand, absorb what was going on around you. Study on your own time, the Weather Manual, Airport Procedures, Aircraft types and capabilities, Radio terminology and techniques; memorize the airway system and abbreviations for the reporting points and operating stations, airports, and aircraft types. When you thought you had a handle on it all, you requested an examination date with the downtown office to write the exams one at a time until finished. The next step was to get a Radio Telephone license so you could use the Radio equipment.

THE ATTRIBUTES OF GOOD CONTROLLER WERE AND STILL ARE:

1. Common sense & Stability

2. Flexibility & Good Judgment

3. Maturity, Alertness, Decisiveness

4. Ability to work Individually or as a Team Player

5. Reliability

6. Memory Retention & Loyalty

7. Self Confidence, Self Control, Integrity

8. Good Voice Projection

9. Leadership Qualities

10. Responsibility & Initiative

11. Ability to Work under Stress

12. Gregarious

13. Ability to think in an abstract three dimensional environment.

Winnipeg Tower used a board with large numbers on the outside of the tower facing the runways. This was for the benefit of the Nordo aircraft to see which runway was in use. When the wind direction changed someone had to run out and change the numbers, no matter what the temperature, it could often be -30° Fahrenheit.

Usually everything in the Tower went along tickety boo, until bad weather moved in or a power failure occurred. Emergencies always seemed to happen when the weather was bad or some aircraft had a radio failure. Backhoes working around the airport area often would dig up cable and cut off the tower landlines. Due to the numbers of aircraft that would be in the air using VFR plus the scramble was on to get back to base, also the navigation flights would return and this would produce a stack. Some were stacked on beacons and some the range. VOR's were not in use in Canada, and there was no radar.

Aircraft on the bottom of the stack naturally got first chance to the approach, but when an aircraft iced up, or had fuel problems, it usually came barreling right on down through the whole mess. This stacking system sounded straight forward and should work - 10 minutes between let downs, if all Military, otherwise fifteen minutes. So when the aircraft was cleared for an approach, it had fifteen minutes to carry that out. In the tower the noise level was high due to the poor acoustics and the row of individual speakers along the front of the console. One speaker for each frequency and several would be in use at one time.

At times the ground visibility would be so bad; the ground controller could not see the aircraft or vehicles on the taxiways. The old hand signals were then used between ground controller and airport controller to signal each other about different occurrences. Once an aircraft called for taxi instructions and the controller gave him the works (wind direction, speed, time, altimeter and direction) to get to the button of the runway. A little later after the controller strained his eyeballs, but couldn't see anything, he asked for his approximate position. The aircraft said it was still in the hangar and would be starting up shortly!! Everyone howled with laughter at this, but the ground controller was too busy, and just let it slide.

The Tower quite often got phone calls from Realtors, who had houses on the market near the airport. The Realtor wanted to know the wind direction and which runway was in use. If runway 36 or 32 were in use, there was no sense in taking a prospective client around because of the noise levels on those approach paths.

One Realtor actually wanted us to hold traffic to another runway for about 30 minutes, so he could take his client to see a house on the approach path to runway 36!!

U2 Plane Gary Powers Spy Plane

(This is the plane that Gary Powers flew and was shot down in Russia, I believe in 1962)

Delta Airlines DC3_Canadian Aircraft

Thunderbirds T33 Primary Trainer RCAF

Air Traffic Control
- Book 2

In all narration there is only one way to be
clever. And that is to be exact

—Robert Louis Stevenson.

Once the exams were completed successfully, it was not yet time for celebrating. There was another six months training in the Tower and the Centre. If you passed the medical requirements, and performed to the satisfaction of two or more of the veteran Controllers, plus the Chief of the Unit, your license was endorsed for that unit only. Every move and every word you uttered was monitored by the licensed Controllers on whose shifts you worked until you earned their confidence that you could handle anything in the heat of the battle. There were about six Controllers training at Winnipeg at this time, using the same methods, but as aviation was moving ahead rapidly, this method was not working. A mass hiring program began in late 1955. A school was set up in one of the old hangar buildings in Winnipeg, plus another one in Ottawa.

Of the group that I trained with, six stayed in Winnipeg, two went to Regina and I moved to Saskatoon.

There were two Controllers in Saskatoon who had applied for Winnipeg Tower and Centre. They were waiting for me to arrive, and check out so they could move on to Winnipeg. The Military training programs in Canada were stepped up, plus their commitment to NATO training brought hundreds of students from various NATO countries around the world.

The first Trans Canada Air Lines DC-3 flew into Saskatoon from Winnipeg on July 1, 1947 to begin a direct daily commercial passenger service linking the Hub City with transcontinental flights between Toronto and Vancouver.

Saskatoon had just christened a brand new terminal building with a symbolic new tower sitting on top. This was a big improvement from the old wooden structure built for the air force in the 1930's.

The air force had their own flight planning office, weather observers and forecasters, firefighting crews and maintenance equipment. Married quarters (PMQ) and a complete Military base had been built. The main traffic at that time were the B25 (Mitchell), and the C45 (Beechcraft). Mitchinson's Flying Service had a Green Hornet (PA 23). There were a few DC3"s around and various other light aircraft, and the air ambulance. Trans Canada started flying North Stars into the airport twice a day.

There were two runways approximately 6,200 feet by 200 feet wide. The light aircraft used the grassy areas, while the heavier aircraft used the hard surface. We were able to accommodate more planes this way. The light aircraft would be on final alongside the Military, and one landing on the runway, and the other on the grass. Radios in all aircraft were not a requirement so the light gun was used extensively. There was a flare gun also, but the only time I saw it used was in Winnipeg. A Military aircraft had lost its radio and when two planes were lined up for the same runway, and too close, the Tower fired a red flare to signal the Nordo (no radio) to overshoot. Two Controllers worked the day shift, one evening, and one midnight shift. The Chief of the Saskatoon Unit was also a working Controller, who had to work a shift the same as the other Controllers. In total there were six Controllers.

The men and women staffing the Control Centers and Towers across Canada are a highly skilled and dedicated group. There is between them, and the Pilots they watch over, a bond of mutual trust and respect. Canadian Controllers are trained and employed by the Federal Department of Transport, later called Ministry of Transport, and now Transport Canada, which is also responsible for the installation and maintenance of all navigation and radar facilities including terminal buildings and runways.

Saskatoon starts booming

The old terminal building was occupied by the radio range operators and the flight planning office, with the tower personnel in a small box two floors higher. The whole structure was not as large as farmer's chicken coop. By comparison, the new building was like a breath of fresh air.

Shifts often involved working in the dark radar room for two hours, then move to the tower in the bright sun for two hours; then take a break and go back into the dungeon for the rest of the shift. This was very hard on the eyeballs, and they would water for the first 15 or 20 minutes, even with sunglasses on. In the summer, after working in the cool dungeon and stepping outside to go home, the heat would almost knock you onto the pavement.

The visibility from the Saskatoon Tower was, for the most part, unlimited. On an average day we could see 25 miles; at night we could see 40 to 50 miles at higher levels (25,000 and above). We could see 100 to 150 miles. Saskatoon was recorded as having the most "clear flying days" in all of Canada.

There was this phenomenon, on the horizon every morning around 10 a.m. Everyone has heard of the garage on the desert, but nothing so elaborate on the prairies. The combination of the tower at 70 feet high and the sun rising in the east would create a mirage on the western horizon. Churches, buildings, roads, rivers, and even the town of Borden (Borden was 30 miles west of the airport) would become visible. Some days we could see the automobiles crossing the Borden Bridge.

1956 saw the great influx of new Controllers. Military and civil aircraft were growing in numbers at a rapid pace. The airways and the areas around the airports were becoming increasingly busy. The staff of six at Saskatoon grew to twelve in the next two years. Training became a priority at each control tower in the Region.

Our radio equipment was the old tube type transmitters and receivers. Radio ranges were the main navigation aid plus two ILS systems at the airport. VHF was the popular band for aircraft with radios and was used exclusively by the air carriers. The Military began installing UHF in their jet aircraft, so the tower controller was saddled with split transmissions to the Military and civil aircraft. The Military were never, ever, required to install VHF in the aircraft that would be operating in and out of a civilian airport. So the airliners couldn't hear the Military conversations with the tower or Center and the Military couldn't hear the civil aircraft transmissions.

This was a sore point with general aviation pilots, and years later would be used by the Francophone Controllers advocating bilingualism in ATC.

The Jet Jock from Cold Lake and ADF fixes

Besides the two main frequencies available, there were two other important pieces of equipment. The Aldis Light gun colors red, green and white, and the VHF/UHF/ADF head installed in the tower. Many hours of practice ADF approaches and lost aircraft maneuvers were carried out each day with the piston and jet aircraft. There was a jet jock from Cold Lake, Alberta, who used to go up north every Sunday morning and call for a fix from Cold Lake, Regina, and Saskatoon, about 25,000 to 30,000 feet. We could hear all transmissions from the aircraft okay, and would be able to get all the bearings as he received them from the other stations. He would then ask us for his position. We had a map of the area under a piece of plastic and with a straight edge drew a triangular fix. This would take a couple of minutes, then we would try to pick a prominent lake or distinguishing mark for him to identify. Our fixes were generally very accurate and the ADF became a reliable piece of equipment in the days ahead.

The ADF was used considerably for the next few years until radar was installed in 1958. Small aircraft, not sure of their position, or requesting a steer to the station were quite common occurrences. ADF let downs for jet and piston aircraft were set up, and was standard everyday practice. A no compass procedure was used one day by Bob Power when a T33 flying from Winnipeg to Saskatoon got too close to a thunderstorm near Yorkton. His compass became unserviceable, and the weather at Saskatoon was 1,000 feet overcast with alto-cumulus to 20,000 feet so a no compass letdown in the southwest quadrant was initiated by Bob, and the cloud breaking procedure carried out with a perfect landing on Runway 08.

The UICP (Unit Instrument Check Pilot)

The UI CP (Unit Instrument Check Pilot) school was in full swing now and the C.F.S. (Central Flying School) had just set up shop at Saskatoon. Every day we would see the sky fill up, and the frequencies jam up with transmissions from students and instructors in the air. There would be C45's, B25's, DC3's, T33's F86's and Harvard's from Moose Jaw NATO training school. A few Cessna and Pipers and a Green Hornet from Mitchison's flying school. Mitch's was the only civil training school in Saskatoon at the time. He was the only guy that could land the tri-pacer on the button and turn off on the taxiways. He did a lot of flying early in the morning before others were even out of bed, and would ask for and get clearance to take off from the ramp. One year Mitch had a display at the Exhibition grounds in the Jubilee building. He had a Cessna 172 on display. Everyone thought that he had dismantled the wings and trucked it to the site, about 7 miles south of the airport. But what really happened was he got up early and flew over the city and landed on Lorne Avenue, taxied into the fairgrounds, then manhandled it into the building.

There was only one problem the men in blue just happened to be in that part of the city, coming out of a coffee shop and they saw the whole thing. They didn't know what law or rule that he had broken, so they phoned the tower to see what regulation would apply. I think when it was all over they fined him five dollars, and let it go at that. There was nothing moving in the whole southeast section of the city except the patrol car, so he wasn't a danger to anyone.

The main workhorse for the Trans Canada airlines was the North Star (DC4). They were given priority for landing and takeoff as much as possible, except in bad weather, they pretty well had to take a number and wait. The jet jocks used to give us a hard time in the mess, about always making Trans Canada number one. They even had a trophy that sat at the back of the bar with a Canadian flag and the words "TRANS CANADA" Number One.

25th Anniversary for Moose Jaw

When Moose Jaw airbase was going to celebrate the 25th anniversary of flying, someone decided that the formation of T-33's lined up in the sky to form the number 25 would be appropriate as a fly past. Under the leadership of Doc Pain and Red Morris and a few others, they would practice each day in separate groups and would go on in designated areas. Finally, the day of glory and all the hard work by these pilots in precision formation flying was here. The aircraft (all 25) rolled out on runway 26 for westbound departure. They would take off, formulate on Route to Moose Jaw, and do one fly-past then over to Regina for a fly-past at their airport, then returned to Saskatoon for landing. ATrans-Canada North Star was inbound from Edmonton, and at 25 miles was asked to proceed and remain well north of the West leg of the radio range. His traffic was 25 T-33's departing runway 26. He said "say that again?" It was repeated and confirmed that the 25 were departing at the same time. The T33's were lined up in groups of five across the 200 foot wide runway and when they started moving. It seemed as though the whole runway was in motion. There were no aborts and the sky filled with screaming T-birds.

When they were at Regina, a new controller was on duty, and because of some traffic that he had at the airport, he asked the formation to do a 360 (a delaying tactic for one aircraft). The formation leader queried the request from the tower, and could not comply, so they turned north and headed for home. When they returned to Saskatoon the T-birds split up into groups of five, called up "3 miles on initial", then split into singles on the break, all landing one behind the other left and right side of the runway. About the third last group came and one aircraft lost its radio, he stayed in the formation and at the break one aircraft got directly below him which he couldn't see. The tower couldn't tell him, and so the two aircraft landed one on top of the other, the nose wheel went through the canopy of the T-33 below him, there was no fire and no one injured, but the two aircraft were severely damaged.

The first aircraft used by Trans-Canada airlines in the 1950's were the North Stars (DC 4), Bristol freighter, DC3 and soon to be followed by the turboprops, Viscount and Vanguard. The Lockheed Electra came on the scene in 1959 and had its first major accident that year when an American Airways flight from Chicago tried to land at LaGuardia, and instead, plunged into the East River, killing 65 people. One of the problems of gathering and transmitting information, by use of voice, something may be missed or misinterpreted. Some Controllers are long-winded and used 10 words when one would do the trick, thus, tying up the frequencies or, if on the landlines tie them up unnecessarily.

Sometimes, a pilot would get a stuck mic button, and some of the cockpit chatter was worth millions of laughs. If one was allowed to re tape the voice recorders, it would have become a better seller than Lenny Bruce comedy. One summer day a terminal controller was vectoring an Air Canada DC 9 around some heavy weather to the west of Saskatoon, and he was keeping the pilot informed of the weather buildups as he was getting close to them. The controller uses the word pips to describe the two CB's that showed on the radar. He said, we have a couple of pips here just to your left, 11 o'clock, 5 miles and the captain came back with "we checked that, and we have a couple back in the cabin section".

Another day, a student was up doing circuits with an instructor, and when on the downwind leg his mic button stuck open. Traffic was heavy at the time, and the controller tried to get the message to him but was not successful. The circuit got thoroughly messed up, but everyone listening got a few chuckles as the student was going through his checklist and the instructor was giving him heck for doing it wrong.

Winnipeg ATC Circa 1950

Air Traffic Control
- Book 3

*He, who knows only his own side of
the case, knows little of that.*

—J. Stewart Mill

Boeing and Douglas started the jet revolution in 1958 with the second generation aircraft Boeing with the 707, 720, 727, and 737 and Lockheed with the L1011. Douglas's answer to the 707 and 727 was the DC-8 and the DC-9.This DC-9 rear engine, T-tailed, twin-jet transport came in four models. The series 10 and 20 would carry up to 90 passengers. The series 20 have a longer wing with a high -- lift device and more powerful engines for short fuel takeoffs and landings. The series 30 will carry up to 115 passengers and a series 40 up 225 in a longer fuselage.

Coming along next, in one form of development, or another, were the Jets of the third generation-the jumbos, the super Jets were wide bodied transports and the long-range SST (supersonic transport). The larger, and faster, aircraft became, the more problems resulting in delays in the air, and on the ground at the airports. With more passengers per aircraft, separation standards where increased to give the controller more breathing room and to increase safety standards with these fast-moving flying machines. There are times when air traffic control seems to have been invented to prove the correctness of Murphy's Law if there is anything that can go wrong it will go wrong.

System changes-System breakdown

Between 1955 and 1957 many changes took place at the Saskatoon airport. The Air Force was increasing their numbers rapidly, CFS and UICP schools moved in. The Military operated their own flight planning office, meteorology and firefighting service. TCA added the Viscount, Vanguard and Super Connie to their fleet. The yellow perils from Moose Jaw would be using Saskatoon as a part of their navigation training. Runway 08 was extended to 8,300 feet. The RCAF installed GCA (only two in Canada, the other installed at Churchill, Manitoba.) Controllers were still being hired at a rapid rate and the staff at Saskatoon increased by about 35. Department of Transport (DOT) installed the first radar in Canada in 1957 at Saskatoon, and was operational, but we were unable to use it because of political reasons like Montréal and Winnipeg were not yet operational, and they didn't want a small town like Saskatoon to get the main thrust of the big announcement. So we were instructed to use it for practice purposes only, and in the event of an emergency we could use it, but reports in triplicate would be required to prove that it was actually an emergency.

For the time being though, all we had was the tower and four positions. Airport Controller was responsible for running the circuits and aircraft inbound and outbound within a 5 mile radius. Ground controller was responsible for all aircraft and vehicles moving on the airport. Position C, it was called this because someone decided that ground control would be A, and Airport Controller would be B. So the ADF position was called "Charlie" and all the ADF approaches, lost orientations, no- compass steers and bearing requests were done from this position: 137.7 kHz. All clearances for IFR traffic were requested from Winnipeg on a telephone. A small strip board was set up between the ground controller and airport controller to handle all the IFR approaches and departures. The system would break down many times due to overloading of the land lines and the number of aircraft that needed the service.

One day Winnipeg and the other stations in Manitoba socked in, but Saskatoon had clear blue skies. Winnipeg Center issued a notam that no more IFR aircraft would be allowed to fly in the Central Region, and one hour prior approval was required for aircraft coming in from Alberta or Ontario. We had C45s, B25s, and T-birds lined up on all the taxiways but could not get off the ground IFR. Some cancelled out and went back to the hangar and others decided to go up VFR and try to do some of the training they had scheduled for the day. There were two important factors that contributed to this dilemma. 1. Winnipeg Center was very reluctant to give up any of their airspace. This would reduce their staff and the importance of their position. 2. Some of the Center staff were just not able to cope with a heavy volume of traffic and would lose the overall picture.

To prove a point on one of those many busy traffic days a Saskatoon controller was attempting to get a departure clearance from Winnipeg and the controller was stalling for time hoping that the aircraft on approach would cancel IFR. Controllers usually gave a short crisp clearance, after the read-back a quick acknowledgment with the "initials" and that was finished. The Winnipeg controller would end a clearance with the phrase "your control subject to 312, 645, and 437"naming all aircraft in the air: so to speed things up the Saskatoon controller broke in at the end of the clearance and said "subject all the inbounds and out bounds". The Center Controllers said quote "that will cover it".

It took a long time and many hours of arguments, even some Controllers went away with hard feelings about the whole thing, but something had to be done to get out of the antiquated mess and system that was being forced upon us. Control of a larger chunk of air space and the right to issue our own clearances was given. It improved somewhat, but the same problem existed on the fringe area and the hand-off points. As an example, there was a radio range at North Battleford about 80 miles west. The Red 6 airway was formed by the West leg of the Saskatoon Range and the East leg of the Battleford range - also there was an airway called R12 formed by the Battleford Northeast leg and the Dafoe Northwest leg intersecting at the Hague bacon about 22 miles north of Saskatoon. To separate traffic in and out of Saskatoon the over traffic would go via R12 and thereby pass Saskatoon with no restrictions. For a pilot to fly R12 from Battleford to Hague he would have to tune in to the Battleford Northeast leg to establish his aircraft on R12 and tune in Hague Beacon on his ADF for a compulsory report by the beacon.

Winnipeg Center insisted that when we received a progress report from an aircraft eastbound by Battleford with an estimate on the next fix (Hague) that we would have to ask him if he was on the Battleford Northeast leg. We were embarrassed to ask because the pilot would always say how else can I fly on Red 12? The disagreement finally came to a head, and the Regional Manager, Claude Brereton, could stand it no longer, and said "this is ridiculous, stop the bickering, and don't ask for such embarrassing progress reports."

Some days the yellow perils would come up from Moose Jaw and do a couple of circuits, land, refuel, have a coffee in the coffee shop downstairs. Then flight plan back to Moose Jaw. These were usually NATO students on a cross-country check-ride, students with an instructor. One day, one of them came up on the frequency, asked for landing instructions and acknowledged with a Roger. The active runway was 14 with a strong wind from the southeast. The Harvard showed up in the circuit going upwind against the grain of the traffic. Traffic was light and the controller tried to tell him he was going the wrong way by several different methods, but the Harvard would just say Roger, meaning that he understood. The pilot spoke a few words in a foreign language that sounded like French. There happened to be bilingual people from Ottawa downstairs in one of the other departments, so I ran down to get him to say a few words and to get the aircraft going the right direction. The fellow from Ottawa obliged and gave the proper instructions to the pilot using our mic. The only thing that came back over the airwaves was "huh"?

The Harvard landed with a tail wind of 30 knot and taxied into the ramp. Someone went down to the aircraft to meet him and try to let him know what we wanted him to do. It turned out he was from Belgium, and didn't understand French. Not too much English either, though, because all they taught the NATO student's was the bare rudiments of what they would be expected to hear from the tower. Everyone had a good laugh about that one, and there had been no harm done.

All the Controllers at Saskatoon at that time were young (in their 20s) and full of piss and vinegar. The heavier the traffic, the more challenge to them and we always jumped into the fold each day with more and more vigor. The tougher the situations became the better. Most of the Controllers were members of the Officer's Mess and we were always invited to take part in the activities on the station. Friday's were always "tufor's" and the day shift would go to the mess for a few. Sometimes a few Controllers and the pilots would start discussing the day's problems and sometimes they would be ironed out over a brew. Sometimes they would get into loud harangues but there was never any fighting or hard feelings afterward.

One CFS instructor could always be counted on to bring up the subject of the tower taking away his IFR from him when he was on approach and within sight of the controller. VFR conditions at the field, nice blue sky, no chance of becoming IFR after the approach. To accommodate all the aircraft on approach, it was a rule of the air that the controller could "put the inbound over" to accommodate the next IFR aircraft to commence his approach. Usually there were so many other aircraft in the circuit VFR that the inbound was often given the overshoot and to join the circuit downwind. If he intended to land, or if it was the active runway the controller would try to fit him in for a full stop landing or a touch and go.

Quite a few Controllers would take their work home with them, worry about the day's events, and try to figure out where they made mistakes and how they would have done it if they had another chance. All their decisions had been made on the spur of the moment, and they always tried to make the best judgment that they could. Things didn't always work out to everyone's satisfaction, tapes would be replayed and the after casters would go to work and tell a controller what he should have done. The controller knew better than anyone what he should have done, but in the heat of battle, that was the best he could do.

Some Controllers that couldn't hack it would be put in non-operating positions. A sort of keep him out of everybody's hair and he won't get in trouble. One controller had a heart attack at the ripe old age of 32. Another young controller committed suicide in his late 20's. Some could take the pressure and some could not. Some would drink their troubles away. One controller used to get up at 6 a.m. and tried to prepare himself for the day's work, but would break down and run into all kinds of problems, and run-ins with other Controllers he was working with. He had to be released, but not until after a lot of complaints from the Human Rights people. There was a controller at one of the other stations in the Region that finally broke. He was an excellent controller and no one would have thought that he would break, but they picked him up one day walking down one of the runways. A maintenance vehicle was dispatched. When someone saw him from the tower, he said. "He was just picking up beer bottles and he thought he was on the highway."

There were excellent Controllers and there were some not so excellent. I felt the pressures of the workplace myself, but was fortunate to have a relief valve. I didn't know it at the time that it was keeping my sanity while others were having a hard time to cope. I had joined a small group of dedicated men at the YMCA when I first came to Saskatoon. When I first noticed them they would be sitting at the edge of a tumbling mat, side by side with an instructor sitting in front of them. I watched them work out and noticed that one of the Judoka was older than the rest. He was 42 years old. I was 29 and thought that I would be too old for rough workouts like the one that I had just witnessed. After talking to the group, they had convinced me that I could handle it and to come out and practice with them. The poundings that I would take during the next 18 years were a perfect way to unload the day's problems of work. I could work out three times a week, sometimes on Sunday and go to work feeling fresh as a baby.

The early days in the control tower were exciting, because every day was different and you didn't know what to expect next. At peak periods, the Controllers would have to look after as many as 15 to 20 aircraft all within a 10 mile radius of the airport, all on the same frequency it was pretty hairy, with planes practicing landing techniques and crossing one another's flight paths on the runways. One controller had been in the control position for about an hour and had a good handle on the situation, but the odd time, two would get closer than he would like. He was running C45's and Mitchell's in the circuit on runway 32, the runway was 6,200' x 200' wide, so there was lots of room for two aircraft on the runway at the same time. Our separation standards where for only one at a time and we could run them one behind the other, one touching down at the end of the runway, if the other one on the runway had started his roll usually about halfway down. We would also have a circuit of T-birds on the crossing runway, and the timing had to be right or we would call for an overshoot. One controller had a C45 on the runway and a B25 about a quarter of a mile on final and could see it would be too close so gave the overshoot for the B25, but he was committed to land and the B25 past the C45 right on the runway.

The Air Force understood the problem of too many aircraft for the air space and was willing to let the separation tighten up a bit, but not quite that much. Everything was in motion and the controller had to keep a mental picture as it was continually changing, but there was no way to stop the clock as they do in the training schools and study the problem. The tower was open 24 hours a day and the Air Force would night fly two or three times a week until 3:00 or 4:00 am in the morning. The Controllers change shift about 11:30 p.m. There was one controller who used to work by the clock that is he would not arrive for a shift until on the exact minute. Most Controllers came early and had a 10 to 15 minute briefing, "Mandatory" before starting the shift. Controllers were forever playing tricks on each other. Some could take it with a laugh and others could not.

This nice summer evening, the evening controller had about 15 C45's and B25's and a couple of Piper's and Cessna's in the circuit and flying locally. At about 20 minutes past the hour, he asked the Air Force aircraft to leave the circuit for a while and they were only too happy to do so. This left about four light ones in the circuit when 11:30 p.m. came around. The tardy controller came bounding up the spiral staircase to the tower and almost out of breath skipped to the back of the tower and put down his lunch-bucket and went to the duty controller and said "I got the picture" which meant he had the traffic picture and the duty controller could go home. So the controller got up put his sweater on and said goodnight and went down to the bottom of the staircase, opened the door at the bottom and let it shut to sound as though he had left. He sat at the bottom of the stairs waiting for the Air Force aircraft to start reporting back for landing instructions. Well, all pandemonium broke out when they started calling in. The controller at the bottom of the stairs couldn't control himself for laughing and went on back up to bail out the other controller. Needless to say that was the last time that he ever came in late, or jumped into a position before he knew what was actually there.

Saskatoon Terminal 1950

Roy at Controls

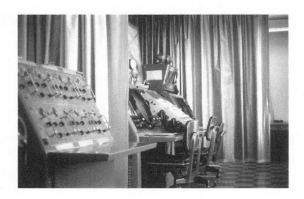

ATC-YXE Terminal – 1950's Arrival, Flight Data & Departure Control

Saskatoon New Terminal 1955

Saskatoon Terminal Control 1960's

Air Traffic Control
  - Book 4

1956-59 - Saskatoon

Communications occasionally broke down between pilot and controller. We would have a number of wheels up landings when aircraft had gear problems. Sometimes a jet would have a flame-out and land on the runway okay, if not they would land on the grass in the infield. The T-birds practiced flame-outs every day from altitudes of 25,000, so that they could practice relighting procedures. The odd one could not get a relight and so would come down for a landing on the runway, they head to reporting positions. They called high key, which was their highest point over the field on the descent to the runway. The next report was at low key, which was a high position downwind for a landing on the chosen runway.

A NATO student in one of those yellow perils from Moose Jaw came up one day and when on final approach, the controller noticed that his gear was not down. He gave him several warnings and the student acknowledged each time with a very cheerful "Roger", and meticulously brought his plane in for a perfect landing; sans wheels. It was only after the pilot walked away from the aircraft that we could see that he was from the Turkish Air Force. I guess you would call it a failure to communicate.

In the control tower, we had a ringside seat on everything that was new and came onto the ramp area in front of the terminal building. The first passenger jet was de Havilland and a comet - a beautiful plane, and it attracted a lot of attention. Another big attraction was the arrival of a Russian TU 104 jet passenger en route to Abbotsford air show. As soon as the word got around the station the Russian jet was coming, the jet jockeys scrambled for other airplanes to get in the air and have a close look at it. They didn't get that close, because they couldn't keep up with it anyway. But they were also warned to keep at least 10 miles from it. The security on the ground was heavy, and the refuel arrangements were kept a secret. The fuel was trucked in by McKay transport and samples were taken continuously while being refueled.

There was a large crowd from the Ukrainian population of the province to greet the aircraft and its doors were opened for the public to see for about an hour. The Controllers had spread the word to their buddies at home on days off, so that they could see a once in a lifetime event. We took turns going down to walk through the aircraft and actually see inside. The plane had exposed rivets and had a sleek, speedy look to it from the interior of a 19th century railway train, even to velvet curtains on the windows. The seats were covered within, all of green velvet material. The plane didn't look as though it had been built for comfort, rather to hold as many passengers as possible.

One evening it was very dark and there were two Controllers on duty. Traffic was light, and one of them took a break and went downstairs. A short while later there was a loud crashing noise on the tower window, it scared the controller on duty and he phoned the RCMP (the airport was under RCMP jurisdiction). They came out and inspected the window and decided it was a rifle shot fired from somewhere on the roof below. There were reports to be filed and the new window cost about $600. It was never proven or owned up to but was assumed to be caused by another controller (the one on the break), who thought he would throw a pebble up to arouse the controller on duty.

There was a controller named Orville, who carried a normal sized lunch bucket and a thermos of coffee. Everyone had to bring their lunch and eat on the job, because there was no coffee shop in the building and you couldn't leave the position anyway, because there was no one to relieve you. Through the course of a day Orville would open his lunch bucket and pull out a little morsel and would pour a small bit of coffee in the lid of the thermos. He had it proportioned exactly through the years of training to make his lunch last till shift change time. Even though he didn't eat any more than anyone else it seemed as though he had a bottomless bucket and was always eating. The other Controllers used to kid him about making a stop at the Dairy Queen on the way home from work to tide him over till he got home and could have something to eat.

One Sunday morning when things were quiet and there was no Air Force flying on the weekends except the transients coming and going, one controller decided to take a walk and get some fresh air. There were just two of them on duty that day. He walked over toward the maintenance building and spotted the truck parked outside the building. It was pointing towards the tower and the keys were in it. The devil got to him and took over, and he got in the truck and revved up the engine with the windows down, he made a transmission to the tower pretending to be an aircraft about 10 miles southeast of the airport and asked for landing instructions. The noise sounded like a regular transmission from an aircraft so, the tower controller didn't suspect anything. Martin shut off the engine closed the truck door and walked back to the terminal building. He waited a little longer then went up the stairs to the tower he got briefed from the other controller and said he had the picture and would look after things. The other controller was quite worried about this airplane that had called some time ago on the ground control frequency and sounded like he may have had engine trouble. He had already called Winnipeg and alerted search and rescue so didn't want to leave the tower until he had seen what the ending would be. Martin finally put on the stern look and ordered the other controller to leave and have a break, and that he would look after things. As soon as the other controller left tower, Martin phoned Winnipeg to straighten the whole mess out. There was no harm done and it had been caught before things got too far gone.

Tom was a good controller and he was very conscious about his appearance. He had to work the midnight shift, then catch an Air Force DAK on to Winnipeg right after shift in the morning. So he had come to work with his lunch and a small suitcase for his trip the next day. When the traffic died down about 3:00 a.m. in the morning, lights were turned down in the tower and the field lights turned off. Controllers were known for their adeptness for sitting in a chair and falling asleep for 40 winks when time was dragging in the wee hours of the morning. But this guy had it all, he took off his good clothes and hung them neatly upon the back of the chair and put on a pair of pajamas so that the pants wouldn't get creased. Only thing was the controller coming on duty in the morning came early and caught the other controller still in his pajamas .Marty does this ring any bells?

As a controller in Winnipeg, who would quite often fall asleep right at the control board. They usually work in pairs in the Center, one on radar and one coordinating on the board and the phone. Another controller would be working away and turn to ask Don for some information, but Don would have fallen asleep. So one evening Don fell asleep in his chair and when the midnight shift came in one of the Controllers went over to the door and told them to be very quiet because Don was asleep and they wanted to play a trick on him. So the midnight shift came in, got briefed and evening shift went home, except Don was still asleep. When he woke up it was two hours past his shift time and he was very angry at the others for pulling off this trick. He didn't think it was funny at all.

There was a saying in the Center "level board-level mind", when some Controllers would attempt to keep the strips in each bay of his control position level by putting empty strip holders where needed to level off the strips into each bay. There was one controller who took great pride and great pain to keep his board level at all times viewed in one bay. One of the more mischievous Controllers took a long time, one evening shift to set up the board for Jack coming to work on the midnight shift. He runs thin string through the strip holders in such a way that when one was pulled out the whole bunch would tumble down. The trick was to get them set up so that he would hold the right one. They put all the strips level except one, in one row, set up from the rest. This was to be the one he would pull. Sure enough, when Jack came in and was briefed everyone was waiting for the big thing to happen. And just as though on cue, Jack reached up to move the strip out of place, and the whole board came tumbling down. Jack didn't think that was very funny at all.

As traffic grew and the number of Controllers increased, so did the system of handling the traffic more efficiently. The complexity of the mix of different types of aircraft and the volume at Saskatoon airport dictated the terminal approach control should be set up. This operated for a while right in the tower, but the noise level and Controllers bumping into each other made it necessary to move the approach control unit downstairs to another room. There were three positions with two radar units. Approach control on the left, data coordinator in the Center and departure controller on the right. To see the radar properly the room had to be kept as dark as possible. Curtains were put up on tracks around each position, and then all windows to keep the light out.

Before the radar was to be commissioned for use it had to be flight checked for blind spots and resolution accuracy. A specialist, Jack Dodd was sent out from Ottawa to oversee the flight check procedures. There was no air conditioning in the room and the heat generated from the two radar sets made it very hot in the room. One controller working on the flight checks had to strip to his shorts to feel comfortable. About a week after Jack had been in Saskatoon, he was taken to the hospital suffering from dehydration. We used to complain about the dryness of the room, but the officials from Winnipeg said that we played the humidity thing up too much. Controllers would go home at the end of a shift with a sore throat and often end up with a cold. We installed a small humidifier card to test the humidity in the room and it read "dryer than the Sahara Desert." We finally had an air conditioner installed. Not for our benefit, but they had found out that the equipment was going squirrely because of the heat, and so it was installed for the benefit of the radar. It was the only room in the terminal building with air-conditioning and was resented. There was one radio technician who used to come in the room and smoke a big fat cigar, just to make it not enjoyable for the controller. There is another fellow who was the electrician's helper who thought the Controllers were overpaid and babied too much and had very few good words to say about us. He used to walk through the room when we were busy and no one noticed but he would walk into the room where the air conditioner was installed and turn it on full blast and leave. The Controllers would notice how cold it was getting and realized after a while that it would happen each time Mike would walk through the room. So rather than get in a hassle with Mike, whenever he walked through we would wait a reasonable time and go to the other room and readjust the air conditioner.

On the front of the radar consoles there were two small containers for holding a soft drink and the other one for cigarette ashes. Most Controllers were in the process of quitting the habit but there was a few still enjoyed it. Fred was a heck of a nice controller and he smoked a pipe. A stomped out cigarette, or dead pipe ashes seemed to smell the worst. Sitting in the darkroom, everyone usually wore a white shirt and tie and Fred would move into one of the positions and clean his pipe. There is a pile of paraphernalia that went along with him when he changed positions. His pipe, pouch of tobacco, cleaner and tamper and jackknife. He would take off the bowl of the pipe and blow real hard through it to clear it out. Being dark, no one would notice till they got home and the wife would ask what all those oil spots were on our nice clean shirt.

When the Air Force was not flying in, the traffic was light and we could push back the drapes and open the windows for some fresh air. There were three positions in radar and three in the tower and each controller would work one position for two hours then rotate, so that by the end of the shift everyone would have worked all positions. One day Joel Nelson was working in the tower and he found an extra phone handset. He tied a rope on it and lowered it to the window of the radar room. They got a call on the squawk box that someone was wanted on the outside line. It was now time for shift rotation and I had to go to the tower and Joel would come to the radar room. I had purposely left the window wide open and the drape opened so that a person could step out onto the roof. After some time had elapsed and I knew that Joel was in the room, I got a bucket of cold water and took it outside the tower near the railing above the radar room. Controllers were notorious for looking through the binoculars at various sites around an airport when things weren't busy so it was not uncommon to see a couple of lovers in the car in the parking lot. I hollered down to Joel to take a look at the couple making out in the parking lot. When he stepped out the window to go across the roof and have a look, I let the pail of water go and got Joel pretty wet. Well Joel came steaming up to the tower and was red with anger, we were laughing so hard that Joel couldn't contain his anger and he broke out laughing although I would be sure someday down the line he would catch me to even the score..

Russian TU104 – 1959 in Sask

Approach Control Tower in Sask

(Far left, Kjell Sundin, 2nd left Roy Cushway – Controller, 3rd Roger Stone, Chief using Approach Control, 4th Ted Pischak looking through Binoculars)

Air Traffic Control - Book 5

Here are a couple of stories that I wrote, of my experiences while at Goose Bay. The three D's don't remember them. Some are funny now, but that was the way it was then, so can't do anything about it now. Our time at Goose was very exciting and went by quickly. Wouldn't want to do it again, but I also am glad that we didn't miss it.

—Roy

Chance of a Lifetime

In the spring of 1960 a request for volunteers for Goose Bay Labrador came to our unit. Normally this station was staffed by Montréal, Moncton, Toronto and Ottawa. When they were running out of volunteers at these units they called on Controllers from the Control Centres. Goose was a Control Centre and handled Military and civilian traffic, oceanic control, domestic control, and Northern control. Saskatoon was an IFR terminal control unit and so qualified as a source to draw personnel to fill the two-year terms. As soon as the Chief, Roger Stone asked me "if I was interested." I said. "Yes", even though I hadn't consulted with the family, and most important of all, the good wife. I didn't want to miss out on an opportunity for a once-in-a-lifetime experience. The excitement of going to an isolated unit in northern Canada was overwhelming and I forgot to phone the wife and tell her the news. Roger phoned her and said "are you packed yet"; he didn't know that I hadn't had time to tell her, so Jean was more than surprised to hear of this new venture. Our family was very young, our daughter, Dorothy was four years old and the twin boys, Dave and Doug were just 10 months old.

After some frantic digging through books at the public library to find out more about this place Goose Bay we discovered that there is no defined border between Labrador and Québec and the colored lines on the maps are just that. Depends on who you ask (a Newfie or a Québécois) the border will always be different. Goose is on the same parallel as Saskatoon, even though it doesn't look like it on the map. Weather wise it is called a catchall of the low pressure systems that move across Canada from west to east. Low pressure systems seem to hang around for weeks until they die there. Goose is the only place in Canada where a Canadian had to clear Customs on arrival and departure, even though it was part of Canada. Because of the large American base, there was concern that too much smuggling would be going on. A lot of smuggling went on at Goose, but it was small potatoes compared to today's standards. Small items like household goods, fresh food products, cigarettes, liquor, typewriters and parachutes were among some of the items.

Trans Canada Airlines advertised "we will look after your young ones during the flight on our aircraft while you enjoy your trip in comfort". We reserved a seat on a Super Connie, from Saskatoon to Toronto and the packing of household goods began in earnest. There was a limit of 500 pounds that we were allowed to ship. Only the necessities for the flight were carried in two suitcases, the rest went by truck, train and steamship.

First Disaster

The trip from Saskatoon to Winnipeg was a disaster. The twin boys had filled their diapers within minutes of each other which coincided with the serving of the noon meal. The Connie was full and we only booked two seats, carrying the baby's on our lap because the stewardess's would be looking after them while we had our meals. This of course isn't how it worked out. We had to struggle with a plate of food and the baby with a dirty diaper on our lap. We tried to take turns, one looking after the young ones while the other ate. Jean ended up eating a cold dinner. Did you ever try to change a diaper on a crowded airplane? Well the super Connie was notoriously crowded seating at best. They had three abreast seating, so we occupied two seats. I don't think some of the other passengers enjoyed their trip as much as they might have if we hadn't been there.

Diapers then were made of cotton, and were not like the disposable type around today. After struggling for quite awhile in my seat trying to get the smelly job done, I spotted an empty seat at the rear of the aircraft. So we were able to take them down there, one at a time and get the job done. I had complained of the lousy service after the trip, to the Head Office of Trans Canada in Montréal. There was a sympathetic reply and hoped it would not happen again. We flew from Toronto to Montréal on a Vanguard; these were fairly new aircraft then and there was lots of room. The only passengers seem to be Trans Canada employees then heading back to Montréal. The next day was another disaster with the airline.

Second Disaster

The flight from Montréal to Goose Bay would be on a North Star, and we had asked for pre-flight boarding. A nice young stewardess met us at the doorway and escorted us to the aircraft. We sensed something wrong as soon as we boarded the airplane, there was no one else on board not even a captain or co-pilot, and the floors had just been scrubbed and were still wet in places.

The stewardesses helped us off with the clothes and get settled in the seats. I asked if she was sure this was the right aircraft, and if it was really going to go to Goose Bay? She was positive, because that was the flight she was working and she had the right aircraft. As time slipped by, it became more and more apparent that in fact we were on the wrong airplane. A frantic call on one of the ground vehicles, and we were whisked away to another aircraft that already had started engines and was leaving the ramp. Everything stopped and we were hustled on board, so much for pre-flight boarding.

Arriving at Goose Bay, our new Home for 2 years

We were met at the Goose Bay airport by Cy Thorley, an ATC supervisor at Goose. He showed us where to go and what we should do to get settled in the new place. This was the procedure for every family arriving at Goose, because there would be a whole lot of things that you wouldn't expect to have to contend with at the isolated post.

The house that we would be living in for the next two years was a duplex, two-story, all hardwood floors and beautiful maple furniture. All the dishes and silverware and small appliances were supplied. Cy gave us some canned food and some fresh food to get us going for a couple of days. Jim Conway, my friend from Saskatoon and who had transferred to Winnipeg lived next door. He came over and gave me 100 pound drum of Starlac powdered milk. We got the routine for ordering our supplies from Montréal to arrive at Goose Bay before the last ship arrived in the harbor. Then we could pay all these guys back when ours arrived. It took a while to get settled with the routines. But everybody said that "you stay loose on the Goose". The fast pace of the big city disappears and things come to a grinding halt. No more rushing here, rushing there. Drive here; drive there, because there were only a handful of cars. Travel was by Shanks pony, bus or a bicycle.

For the life of our stay in Goose Bay, we would have many more of these thrills, as anyone who has raised a family will be well aware of.

Our youngsters were at the age that everything had to be put away, because it would otherwise be put in the mouth or dragged to the edge of the table and pulled off. One item that we had not considered was a small black-and-white 14 inch TV. One day Harold the storekeeper was at the house doing an inventory in the kitchen. I was at work and Jean was busy in the kitchen. Dorothy was at school, and the twins were busy as usual in the front room. Good old Dave, miraculously somehow pulled the TV off the table and it hit the floor with a bang right on the screen side. It scared Harold and Jean and of course, it scared the heck out of Dave. The peculiar thing about it though, was that he didn't get a scratch and the TV didn't get broken. Harold put the TV back on the table and it was still working as though nothing had happened.

The Airport

The whole airport was divided into three main parts. The RCAF area which included a swimming pool and a curling rink, with a row of hangers called a hanger line, as well as living quarters for their personnel. The DOT area where there were was personnel from meteorology, air radio, and air traffic control. The USAF area, by far the largest and most elaborate. This was like a small city plopped in the middle of a sandy plateau covered with Jack Pine, black flies and mosquitoes. There was 20 miles of road. It started in a small hamlet like place called Happy Valley where the native Newfoundlanders lived, and stretched to Northwest River with the roads leading to the three main bases. Bus service was excellent. Operated by the DOT the regular runs were to the RCAF base and to the Hudson Bay store. The main purpose of the bus though, was to take the workers to the Control Centre, about 4 miles from the living quarters. We met a lot of good friends at Goose and we will talk about some of them later on. Some were from Happy Valley, some from the US airbase and RCAF base and of course from the Canadian side. The place was like the League of Nations as far as a sampling of personnel from across Canada was concerned. There was someone representing each Province and all had different stories to tell, about how it was done at home. The type of aircraft was quite different than most were used to at their home base. There were various USAF and British aircraft operating from one of the largest airfields in the free world. There were civilian air carriers that were in the midst of changing aircraft from the old DC7's, Britannia's and super constellations and DC6's to the jet type of DC8 and Boeing 707's.

Doing good is the only certainly happy action of a man's life.

The oceanic traffic was the most interesting and informative to work. Of all the accents that I ever heard, the Air France was probably the most exciting to listen to. The pilot would call up the Center with "Goose Santer this is Aayyeerr Froonnzze Zayero Zayero won". The BOAC was probably next for a colorful voice. "Gayoose Centaahrr this is Speedbuurrd tywoo tywoo zeeero, owevayeehrrr". Some of the other airlines were JAL (Japanese Airlines), El Al (Israeli Airlines), Lufthansa, Scandinavian, Irish, KLM, Alitalia, Air Canada and all the US carriers.

Over the Pole

Scandinavian Airlines was probably the first airline to circumnavigate the North Pole back in the 1950's. They set up a track called the polar route and were the only airlines to use it for some time. There was very little navigation aids and no communication system when they first started. Their first stop coming off the North was Winnipeg and they were only allowed to pick up fuel and meals and dispose of their garbage. No passengers were to deplane or board. Air Canada made sure of that. They "Air Canada" held a pretty tight rein on who could fly where, and do what, in Canadian air space. We've come a long way Charlie Brown, now with deregulation in the airline industry.

Red Cross Swimming and Scuba

Several of the Controllers that were involved in the Red Cross programs at the local swimming pool were also involved in the scuba diving program. The RCAF had all the equipment including the dry suits. Wetsuits were not invented yet. The pool was standard Olympic sized with a deep end of thirteen feet. Our class was once a week and we would practice checking the regulator and equipment then spending about an hour doing routines in the water. Two of the routines were, donning a blind on the face mask, and have the swimmer perform a series of lost orientations, underwater. The other was to dive down at the deep end and take off the equipment to abandon it on the bottom using the weight belt, and then slowly surfacing breathing out all the time to let out the expanded air in the lungs.

One of the Controllers had missed several weeks of practice, and had come down this night to go through his routine. We were usually left on our own after we passed a certain stage in the training. He put on the equipment and went to the deep end to do the abandon procedure. He went to the bottom, took off his equipment, put the weight belt over it all, took a last breath of air and turned off the regulator. Squatted his feet on the bottom and with a great push off, went speeding to the surface. His lungs almost burst, and it scared him so much that he got out of the water after he got his wits about him, put on his clothes and went home and never came back again. He had been away too long and forgot that he had to ascend slowly breathing out to get rid of the expanded air.

During my workout at the gym on the American side I got to know a lot of fellows and met many more good friends. One of the funny things that I noticed with these guys was that they always had a first name to match someone important. If the guy's last name was Washington everyone called him George even though his name was Harry. If the name was Wayne then his first name had to be John. I guess in a way it was good because if you missed the first name when being introduced to, you automatically called him by some famous name and it would be okay. With my new Eaton's bike, I used to ride to the American base once a month or so, to have a taste of a hamburger or a hot dog, a glass of mechanical cow and an ice cream cone. Mechanical cow was powdered milk mixed in a mechanical mixer and bottled and sold just like bottled milk.

Ritzy

There was a guy on the base named Ritzy and he worked for the DOT radio branch. He was a wheeler dealer and he had an in with a guy on the American side that was supposed to dispose of all the surplus stuff like typewriters, tents, parachutes and small items like that. I think everyone on the Goose on the Canadian side had a typewriter in his house. When it was time for the person to leave he would sell it to another controller because Customs would catch it for sure, on their routine check of all your boxed goods.

The dump was a place that a lot of perfectly good items were thrown. When our "new store Maple furniture" was being replaced, we were not allowed to keep it to bring it home. It would be broken then burned at the dump, although I do know of a couple of Controllers that were successful in keeping a Maple easy chair and sending it home. If a parka was turned in, it would be slashed with a knife so that it could not be used again. Skunky beer would be hauled out to a wide open area and under the watchful eye of the RCMP; a bulldozer would crush every can.

Skunky beer

One year the officer walked away when they were only halfway through the process, and soon as he was out of sight, the rest was saved, and even though it was skunky the guys quaffed it all. On the DOT base in the Squirrel Club there was a small room for a pool table and off to the side was a barber chair. One of the Met guys used to cut hair for fifty-cents (50¢), and if you didn't mind he did a pretty good job. So that kept him in pocket money and saved the guys from worrying about making an appointment on the RCAF base barber shop. Also you could play a game of skittles while you waited. Seemed that the game of skittles started up there and that was the only game that was played, mind you it was a very interesting pastime and the competition was fierce. We usually played for dimes (10¢) and quarters (25¢) if you got knocked out, as with any other game there were the real serious players who would get angry if they lost too many times and then there were the fun players who just wanted to pass the time and have some fun.

Names disappear

The U.S. Military had a payday run to Frobisher Bay, Hope, and a couple of other stations north of Goose. There was usually just a paymaster and a bodyguard and a pilot. So they had invited any Controllers that wanted to make the trip with them, and to see a bit of the North Country. There was a list on the bulletin board in the Centre about two pages long with the names of Controllers wanting to take advantage of this offer. The weather around Goose was usually rainy and low overcast when the low pressure systems from across Canada congregated on the east coast waiting to dissipate. One of the pay runs was coming home and the weather was cloudy with a ceiling about 100 feet and visibility poor. The helicopter tried to make it and got too low for the Mealy Mountains to the south, hit them and disappeared. The search went on till late fall but nothing was found and the search was called off. Of course the two pages of names disappeared in a hurry as the Controllers decided they didn't want to see the North after all.

Northwest River

Sometime during the next spring, a nomad Indian came into Northwest River with a wallet. The RCMP asked him if he could show them where he found it. He took them to the spot, deep in the bush where there was a small lake about 150 feet deep. The water was so clear they could see a helicopter sitting on the bottom. The diving team was brought in from Montréal and they went to the bottom, connected flotation devices to the aircraft and floated it to the surface. The investigation was carried out and all that was necessary was saved and the aircraft was pushed back into the lake to sink to the bottom.

Jim Conway had asked me one day if I would be interested in renting the harbor master's boat and taking a trip to Northwest River for a day. This sounded interesting enough and we made the plans for babysitters, etc. The harbourmaster's only stipulation was that one of his men had to drive the boat. That was okay by us, and so we took off on Saturday morning with our wives and a couple bottles of Newfie screech. It was a pretty rough trip across the bay, about 8 miles across, and when half the screech was gone so were we.

We did manage to visit the Village of Northwest River and Grenfell mission. The ladies shopped in the Hudson Bay store and Jim and I went across the river to the Indian village. I would not have believed it if I hadn't seen it for myself. They all lived in tents all year round and I would swear that about 12 or 15 kids poked their heads out of the tent while we were visiting. There were some very crowded conditions and uncomfortable by our standards. We picked up a puffin made out of sealskin by one of the local natives. Sealskin anything would not sell on the European markets today. When we return to Goose the mother-in-law was a bit upset at our condition, and the fact that we did really have a good time.

The rule on the Goose was that there were no visitors allowed, with a few exceptions. One that was okay, of course was Jean's mother was allowed to visit for two weeks to help with the Twins. A special pass had to be drawn from the airport manager's office, and she liked it so well at Goose she decided to stay for six months. Jean's mother had been looking after her father in North Vancouver and decided to let someone else look after him, and said she was needed at Goose to look after the Twins. The father was getting old and crotchety and it was quite a handful to look after him. We were allowed an extension of the pass and the mother-in-law got a part-time job on the American side babysitting a house while an American family went stateside for a holiday. The rest of the time she spent with us and stayed till we left the Goose.

Some must follow, and some command, though all are made of clay -Longfellow–

The FAM – Not for Me

One of the things that a controller looks forward to when he has been in isolation for a year or more is the chance to go "outside" for a few days and make sure that he isn't getting "stir crazy", let off a bit of steam, then return refreshed and ready to face the day again. One of these outlets that the Controllers had was the gig called a FAM trip. This was to be a familiarization trip with another unit in the Region you are working with and to get a chance to shoot the breeze with the pilot on the way out and on return. Usually on a two-year voluntary tour, the Controllers had the opportunity to fly to Moncton or Halifax to visit their unit. I was on my second year of the tour and had applied for a FAM trip to Moncton; several other Controllers had also applied. There was a controller, who had been on a tour of Goose before, and he had volunteered for a second tour and had just arrived on the Goose. He was a good friend of the Chief, and the Chief had wanted to get a small car shipped in for his convenience. They struck up a deal for this controller to go out on a FAM trip and buy him a small car in Québec or New Brunswick and have it shipped in on the next boat. My FAM request was then turned down.

When this turn of events happened I complained, and the answer I got was that I would be leaving this year and it would be of no benefit to me. Anytime that a controller got a chance to visit another unit, it was to his advantage to absorb as much information of how the different units worked and the equipment that was available in that particular Region. Also he would have the chance to meet other Controllers and exchange ideas and friendships. Not to mention the fact it would be a chance to get to the outside and away from the isolated environment for a few days. This controller that was taking my place had just come in from the "outside". I was not satisfied with the answer that I was given so complained to the controller representative at the unit. He made a written complaint, which the Chief had to answer in writing. His written answer was very vague and very evasive to the question. But the end result was the same big No, his mind was made up and no one was going to change it.

The Best Trip of My Life

I survived the rest of my tour and had accumulated six weeks holidays, which we took after leaving Goose and before starting work again at Saskatoon. Over the two-year tour of duty, I became a good friend of Harold Shiwak and his family and his brother George and Jimmy Learning, and many of the locals that lived in Happy Valley. George was a trapper and a hunter and spent the winters up along the coast of Labrador on his trap lines. He was in his early 30's and Jimmy was in his late 20's. Jimmy worked at various jobs, nothing steady, and was hoping to be able to go to the outside to take a training course in electronics. Harold was a good hunter and trapper also, as I would later find out. He casually asked me one day if I like to fish and camp. Of course this was right down my alley and I responded very enthusiastically. I guess he had no alternative than to invite me on a trip with him, George and Jimmy on the next weekend off. I was so excited about the whole thing that I forgot to ask what food and supplies I should bring. Later that week we got together to plan the trip in more detail and they had everything that we would need so I chipped in on some food, which was actually very little because we're about to learn how to live off the land. All that I needed was a good sleeping bag, and that I already had.

Me and the Wild North

The big day arrived, it was a Friday. Harold picked me up at our place and we drove to Happy Valley to meet the other two. We had two 16 foot aluminum boats, a wall tent, a homemade stove, the food and our duffel bags. Harold and Jimmy went in one boat and George and I went in the other. It was a drizzly day and cool and windy out in the bay. It was about 10 miles to cross the bay and the swells were about 4 feet high. I was riding at the front of the boat with my rain slicker on and keeping an eye on the other boat off to our left. I was also getting a little nervous, as we were taking on some water. George was an expert at handling the boat, as he had done this so many times before. He would ride along the trough and then scoot up to the ridge just before it started to curl and flatten it out, before it had a chance to swamp us. We made it across the Bay safely and once inside the smaller channels and out of the open wind, it was more pleasant even though it was still raining. We traveled about another hour up to the Sabesquachi River to a small island where we pulled in to set up camp.

Sweeping the tent

These guys worked fast, and in about five minutes they had a good fire going and a pot of tea ready while George and I set up the tent. George asked me to "sweep the tent" which I had never heard of before, so he had to explain to me how to do it. This was a wall tent with no floor in it, so the method was to go out and cut the small ends of the fir trees, and then lay them on the tent floor curled side down to make a bed for the sleeping bags. The pine smell in the tent was ecstatic and stayed all the time we had the tent there. The small stove was a rectangular shape about 1' x 2' and 6 inches deep with a draft control and three sections of downspout for a chimney, which ran out through a tin plate sewn in the roof of the tent. We gathered enough small pieces of wood and set them inside the tent near the stove. We left our sleeping bags rolled to keep them warm or until we were ready for bed. There was an iceberg pushed up on the other side of the island and this would be my first lesson on how to get fresh water. We went over to the iceberg and the line where the salt was could be seen at about 4 feet down from the top of the iceberg. That meant that all the top of the iceberg was good clean ice and all we had to do was chip off enough to fill the pot and take it back to the camp and thaw it out. There was another supply of water that had been used before. It was a small hole dugout of the peat moss and with the peat acting like a filter would leave a nice well of clear water suitable for drinking.

We boiled all of our water anyway, but at least it wasn't salty. For two nights this was as comfortable living as any camper would want, or dream of. The small twigs and pieces of wood in the firebox in the tent kept everything nice and warm, and with the aroma of pine, how could anyone not have a good night's sleep? Next day after a hearty breakfast Harold set a snare and Jim and I went out in the boat for a little fishing. At the end of the day we had one rabbit, three trout and one Hungarian partridge. So we had lots of food and these guys sure had the knack of making the best tasting meal I've ever had while in the bush.

My Eskimo snow shovel

Further down the Sabesquashi River, Harold and I stopped on another small island for a look around. The whole area is dotted with small islands and they know every nook and cranny like the back of their hand. As we were walking along the pebbled shore, I spotted what looked like a wooden spoon used by a giant. I picked it up and was carrying it along, with the idea of taking it home. Harold asked me what I was going to do with it. I told him, and he laughed so hard because it turned out that it was an Eskimo shovel. According to Harold when they are hunting and fishing in the winter they make them right on the spot to scoop out the ice chips from the hole they make for ice fishing. When they leave, they discard it and make another at the next stop. I told him I didn't care; I was going to take it home as a souvenir from the camping trip. I did, and it's still in the room in the basement standing by the door, to remind me of our fantastic trip on the Sabesquashi River.

On our return from that trip, we got held up on the north side of the bay waiting for the weather to improve. We then set up camp thinking that we would have to stay overnight. We had heard that not too many days before us, two were drowned trying to cross the same area when it was too rough. The water is about 40°F and so a person wouldn't last too long in it. It would take a little over an hour to get across and it was getting close to cut off time for darkness. The wind let up and we took off, to make it across before dark. I guess everyone at home would have been worried if we had to stay the night on the other side, and not knowing for sure, if we had tried to get across in the poor weather.

Ritzy again

Ritzy was a guy they called "the organizer" and the "Wheeler-dealer" on the Goose. He organized a fly in fishing trip for about 12 of us. We were to take all our own gear and share on the food and booze. The cost of the trip to an isolated lake over the Mealy Mountains was $40 each. This included a return trip on a Twin Otter and two cabins to sleep in, and the use of two boats and a canoe.

Overload

The day arrived for us to meet on the dock in the harbor and sort out our gear for storage on the aircraft. We were down there in plenty of time and when all the gear was piled together. It looked as though we may need a freighter to haul it all. The pilot came down a short while later and started getting the aircraft ready. A couple of the guys from meteorology were heavyweights. The other 10 were medium to skinny guys. There were about 20 cases of 24 beer and a few boxes of hard stuff. As the pilot was working getting things lined up. He noticed us all standing together beside the gear to be loaded. He said. "No way will we get off the water with this load; you guys will have to reduce the load before we can go. So Ritzy says, "Come on guys drink a few of these beers, so we can get this stuff on". He cracked open two flats of 24 beer and they disappeared within a few minutes.

The shuffle

Ritzy went and brought the pilot over to see how we had reduced the load, but he said it was still too much. So we opened another 24, and shuffle around on the dock so that it didn't look so big. The pilot came over and said it looked okay and we started loading it. We did have an overload alright and some of the guys had to sit on gear, because there was no room on the seats. The skies were clear and it was a warm Friday morning. The water was reasonably calm, so after the pre-flight check was finished, we started our route southward down the bay. We could feel the ripple getting faster, but the aircraft wouldn't lift off. It seemed an eternity and finally we skimmed just a few feet above the water for about a mile before we got enough speed to try for some altitude. The aircraft was doing a bit of moaning and groaning and we passed over the Mealy Mountains and began the descent to our lake. It was a beautiful big Lake, about 10 miles across with a small protected bay at the south end. This is where the camp was built and it was well protected from the northwest winds.

We unloaded the aircraft and stowed all our gear in the cabins. I don't think there was any order in picking who was going to sleep where. But everyone picked their spot, and any who didn't of course, got the upper bunks where it would be the hottest. I was in a cabin with Baskin and Wonacott and a couple of guys from air radio and one from meteorology. These cabins were very plain, and plywood outside, 2 x 4 frame, Army bunk-beds with mattresses, table and coal oil lamps, some chairs a few dishes and cooking pots and a cast iron frying pan. Most of the fishing the first day was done from the shore and the fishing was good, there was no limit and we didn't need a license. I guess we were too far north for anyone to worry about little things like that, besides the RCMP had more important things to attend to at the base. We had eaten all the fish the first day, and the trout pulled from the cold water was firm and very tasty, after a short fry in some butter.

Fish flies and Mosquitoes

The fish flies were out in full force during the day. Of course they didn't do anything, except bother you with their noise and you would get the odd one in the mouth. As evening comes on the fish flies go into the woods and the mosquitoes come out, and these are not your average garden variety, they are the big and mean ones. The black flies are around all the time and you get used to them after a while. We had stayed up fairly late the first night playing some "growl". It's amazing how much light the coal oil lamp gives off when it is pitch black outside. The cabins were very warm, and they didn't have screens on the windows so we had to keep the door closed to keep out the pests. There were enough cracks in the floor and walls to let too many in as it was. The second night was like the first except after we turned out the lantern and some time elapsed for everyone to get to sleep, Ritzy sneaked across to our cabin and opened the door just enough to let in the millions of mosquitoes that were sitting around outside. Eventually, everyone was awakened by the mosquitoes then realizing that the door was open. Amazing thing also was that all the booze had disappeared in the first two days. I don't think the mosquitoes were into it, but a few of the guys were pretty heavy drinkers.

The last day of the trip was Sunday, and so we were up bright and early and it was a nice day. The water wasn't any warmer, but that didn't matter because no one had planned on swimming anyway. Fishing was the order of the day and we wanted to bring a few back for the freezer and have some proof that we had actually been on a fishing trip. Four guys had been out around the corner in the bay fishing and they caught quite a few. They had returned already with a beautiful catch of brook trout. Four other guys got in the motor boat and went out for a while. There is a small flat bottomed boat, which would hold two people and it was out around the corner also. Half of the guys were fishing from shore and doing just as good as the guys in the boat. The brightly colored Peterborough wooden canoe was sitting on the shore. I knew enough about canoes that this water was becoming too rough to take it out of the bay.

The flat bottomed boat was empty and sitting on the shore, so I decided to take it out for a row. And I took my fishing rod along, past the bay and around the corner onto the big lake. There was a deep channel running north to south and the current underneath was opposite to the flow of the water on the surface. The waves were getting too big for me and I was getting a bit wet and not really enjoying the fishing part of it, so decided to head back around to point to the protection of the bay. On my way in, two fellows were heading out in the canoe, and I thought to myself that they really must be good at handling the canoe in rough water, because that is where they were headed.

One of the men in the canoe was about 59 years old and the other was about 22. They didn't know each other and each thought that the other knew all about canoes. They both worked for the same company (EPA), one was a mechanic, the other was a gopher, baggage handler etc., and both were fairly new on the Goose. That is probably why they really didn't know each other. Wonacott had cooked up some fish already and baked some potatoes on a fire just outside the cabin. We had just sat down and opened the jacket of the potato and had one small sample of the trout when a cry came out for help.

We dropped everything and ran over in the direction of the trouble. The pilot came running over also to see what the commotion was all about. The canoe had gone too far out in the rough water and the two had been sitting sideways in the canoe and casting their lines. The canoe took the least resistive position in the water and was bobbing sideways to the movement of the waves. It so happened that just as one of the fellows cast his line and the canoe rocked a little, the other one cast his line in synchronization with the first cast and with the movement of the next wave, they went over and upside down as fast as you could blink your eyes. The young fellow had a Mae West life jacket on, the kind that used the CO_2 to inflate it. He must've tried to inflate it but it was only half full. The water was cold, and even keeping the head above water a person wouldn't last many minutes. The older fellow had a different type of life jacket and he stayed on top of the water and another boat got to him and took him over to a small island. They started a fire under way to keep them warm, but he was pretty badly shaken up over the whole mess. The canoe had an anchor on it and so the canoe was at the exact spot where it upset. The pilot called everyone together to plan what to do rather than everyone running around in a frenzied state.

About four of us went up in the aircraft to try and spot the boy from the air as the water was crystal clear. We circled the area that was most likely to be the spot, and covered a large portion of the lake but could not see anything. We returned to the camp. Everyone took a fishhook and cleared off the barbs, put them on a long pole and began dragging along the shore. In the meantime, the older fellow was brought over to the camp and warmed up with blankets and the fire and got into some dry clothes.

There was no luck on our search after about a half an hour and so the pilot said he had better get into the base and inform the RCMP. He suggested that some of the group return with him now so that he would be able to bring the RCMP back with him and when they find the boy, all of them could return with the one trip.

Four of us volunteered to return and we were not to say anything until everybody returned, just in case someone started worrying about the accident being their husband. The question came up of how come we were home earlier than expected and how come all of us didn't come home together? I forgot the story we used but it must've been okay, and the rest of the group were back before dark, so the news is out before the accident. After an exhaustive search for the body, the group that was on the search finally went back to the canoe and the body was floating in the water directly below the canoe in a vertical position caused by the partly inflated life jacket.

For some reason the exact spot where he was, there was no undercurrent and no movement of the water to wash them out into the lake or over to another of the shoreline. This accident hit everyone hard and left a lot of room for thinking. The young boy had not been on the base very long and he had a full life ahead of him, but these things happen and only one can say:

"When near water you should always be alert to the danger that lurks in boats or onshore". When I returned to Saskatoon and our family would be traveling in the isolated rivers of the Precambrian Shield, this was always with me.

Guys Get Bumped for a Load of Manure

Many American aircraft would be traveling between Goose and State side every day, and usually the ones going southbound had plenty of room for servicemen who had a few days off if they wanted a lift to a Military field and take the chance of getting home from there. The only problem was getting back to the base, because the aircraft were almost always full of freight or new personnel for their tour of duty. The U.S. side had beautiful lawns and gardens, trees and flowers, while the Canadian side was just the natural environment. When the Americans build a base they make it a typical American city with all the razzmatazz that goes into the big city life. In order to do this, they had to fly in many tons of black topsoil, grass seed and manure. The standard joke of the enlisted men on the U.S. side was that he had gone home to visit with his family, and when he tried to come back he would get bumped for a load of manure. The Goose Base was considered to be an overseas posting for the Americans posted there.

Farewell

Whenever there was a couple of Controllers' finishing their tour of duty, a farewell party would be organized for several that would be leaving at the same time. The NCO's club seemed to be the best suited for things like this and is there was more room there than any of the other messes. One such party was organized to coincide with a few entertainers from stateside that would be appearing in the mess for a week.

At one of the parties there was a full house of Controllers and service personnel and a sit-down dinner and bar. After the preliminaries were out of the way, the group came into entertaining for a couple of hours. One of the entertainers was supposed to be a memory expert and soothsayer. For the entertainment of the audience he said for every person that would call out the name of a city that they came from, he would name the main streets and important buildings in that city. He started with big cities like New York, Chicago, etc., then the action got fast and hot and there were all kinds of guys standing up and calling out their hometown trying to stump this guy. Don Cameron was a controller from Vancouver Center, and his hometown was Agassiz. Don was about 4 foot 4 standing on his tiptoes. This was not high enough to be seen by the entertainer, so Don was standing up on the back of a folding steel chair. He had hollered the name of Agassiz several times but could not be heard over the room noise, so Don let go of the fellow he was hanging onto and cupped his hands around his mouth to funnel his call directly to the entertainer. Just as he got out the words Agassiz he fell off the back of the chair into a heap on the floor. Don didn't get hurt, but it was the funniest thing we had seen for some time. He got up and brushed himself off and got back up on the chair to try again. He got the guys attention and he had to repeat the name several times and spell it until finally he said it was near Vancouver.

Then the guy names off all the streets and buildings in downtown Vancouver. At that same dinner we had black forest cake and baked Alaska for desert. The waiters came in with two litres of dark rum and poured them both all over the cake and the baked Alaska and began to serve it. When I got mine it was still burning a blue flame on top of the ice cream and it had not started to melt.

Our Happy Valley Friends

Our friends from Happy Valley used to come up to our house and bring a few guitars and a violin and with these instruments and their voices were able to have a good evening of entertainment without the aid of artificial music from the radio or record players. Most of the folk were good singers, and I guess it is natural because I remember my aunts and uncles and cousins on the farm were all good singers because they had no fancy artificial gadgets to entertain for them. Usually someone would start a song and if it was fairly popular or an oldie Goldie, then everyone would sing along with them. It was great entertainment and it made you feel good to be able to sing and talk with each other and socialize.

Time to Go Home

These social gatherings became a tradition about once a month and everyone looked forward to the happy event. It was becoming spring time, and those that were planning their last days on the Goose were getting wooden boxes made up especially for their belongings, that had no doubt accumulated over the two-year tour. Some of course had been there for five to eight years and accumulated it even more. Cy Thornley had been on the Goose for four years and was planning to return to Vancouver Center, after taking a holiday and a tour of the Atlantic Provinces. This was 1962, and the Diefenbaker Government was in power. Cy had made the arrangements through the Regional Office to take his holidays, pack up all his belongings and leave Goose Bay, and instead of coming all the way back to Goose, he planned on picking up his moving expense money and his paycheck in Montréal at the end of this holiday, and on the way back to Vancouver.

The news came out that the Tory government had frozen all civil servants to their jobs and no one was allowed to move. This came out after Cy had already left Goose. We watched the news on the teletype and saw an order issued from Ottawa for Cy to return to Goose, and his return to Vancouver was cancelled until further notice. I would presume that Cy was furious by this time, and there was no way he would come back to Goose with his plans so far advanced. When he went to the Montréal Regional Office they would not give him his money, so he told them to stuff it, and paid his own way back to Vancouver.

I was supposed to be going out to Saskatoon in August and the Unit Chief told me that I couldn't leave because of the new order. I wrote a letter to the Regional Manager for Central Region, and he assured me that my position was vacant in Saskatoon and I could go back, whenever I was ready. So I began making the necessary arrangements. We had to go through an "out routine", similar to the Armed Forces, when you move from base to base. The first and most important of course was with the Bank Manager to make sure that all your loans were cleaned up. The rest were through the several Departments of the DOT to make sure everything was as it should be before you get away from them.

The Chief kept after me, saying that what I was doing was all in vain and that he had scheduled me for the next month's shift in the Goose Centre. I didn't tell him that I had a letter approving my move and in fact, I had my expense cheque, and had it cashed, to make sure no one tried to change anything.

As the days drew nearer to my departure time, the Chief was anxious to receive a teletype message from Montréal Region to stop me from leaving. It never came of course, because the Central Region was responsible for my expenses and Montréal had nothing to say about that, even though I was working in their

Region. We had the usual farewell party on the American side with about three other Controllers leaving at about the same time, but none would compare to the party that our friends from Happy Valley put on for us at the Squirrel Club.

Here was the invitation:

"You are invited to attend a farewell reception to be held in the ballroom of the Squirrel Club on August 8, 1962 officially opening at 8:30 p.m. It will be given in honor of Mr. and Mrs. Roy Cushway. A band is hired for this very special occasion and a gift will be presented. The reception will be given on behalf of local Labrador friends that this couple have made during their stay at Goose Bay, Labrador."

Reception committee:

Harold Shiwak, Jimmy Learning, George Shiwak

This was one of the greatest moments of our life to be accepted in their trust and given such a great and honorable send-off from the Goose. All of our friends from the valley were there and we received a handsome silver serving tray with the inscriptions on the top. "From all your friends in Happy Valley."

The Farewell Party goes on and on

My last working shift on the Goose was a few days before I actually left, but it was a day shift. I think some of the guys had planned on not letting me get home, until they were finished with me. As the day shift bus was on its way from the Center for the last time "for me at least" one of the Controllers suggested that we stop at the International Hotel for a farewell drink. The International Hotel was like the old Military green "H" huts that were so prominent across Canada during the war years. It was owned by a group of airlines that would use it anytime their aircraft were laid over at Goose because of weather or maintenance.

There were four Controllers in our group, and after a couple of rounds we ordered a cab to take us to the Squirrel Club, which was a little closer to home and within walking distance for me. They convinced me that I should go into the club with them for one. One of the fellows (Gayton) with us was from Montréal and was an excellent folksinger. He stayed in the single quarters, just behind the Squirrel Club. As we were having the one he said he had to run over to his place for something. We were having a good visit and reminiscing the past two years on the Goose with Don McCallum from Moncton Center who's hometown was Charlottetown PEI. The other controller was Sid Bower from Calgary Terminal, and his hometown was Regina, Saskatchewan. Sid had been to all parts of the country working in the various towers, Centers, and terminals. Gayton was fairly new in ATC and was working as B stand in the Center.

He soon returned and after a short while I made the announcement that I was going home for supper, it was about five o'clock and would be just in time to help with the kids. The others said, "no way" we are all going over to the officers mess on the American side and have a couple more farewell drinks. I said, that was all very fine, but I do not have a tie. A clean shirt and tie and sport coat was the dress code for the mess. They all carried bolero tie in their pockets for such occasions. Gayton slipped two bow ties out of his pocket and said there was no excuse now. After some talk we ordered a taxi and went to the bowling alleys for a bite to eat and a game of 10 pins. They served drinks there also (I think the only place that drinks weren't served was the workplace). The Americans didn't have a swimming pool because of some rule about being above certain latitude. They were not allowed, and Goose qualified as such a place. That was probably the only thing they didn't have and they were allowed to use the big pool on the Canadian side.

I had never bowled 10 pins, but this didn't seem to matter. We would play Sid and myself against Don and Gayton with Sid bowling first, then Don second. After Don threw his first bowl he went over to the racks and picked up another ball to throw. Sid said, "You can't do that, you have to wait for the same ball to return". They got into a great argument over this point, which really didn't matter in this game of ours, but Sid got so mad that he said he wasn't going to play if we didn't play by the rules. It didn't seem to be a big issue with the rest of us so we finished the game without Sid, had a couple of beers and walked over to the officer's mess.

The bar had all kinds of different beers, and one that everyone seemed to like, and was available, was the Dutch beer called Heineken. We had a few and had a good visit and Sid was his old self again willing to forget the bowling game. We ordered a taxi again and took a couple of dozen Heineken beers to Don's home on the Canadian side. This was a night that the checkpoint gave us a wave and we went through with no trouble.

It must have been about midnight by now and long past my supper time. The mother-in-law was at our place so she could help with the kids I figured to myself. Don's wife was out to Moncton on a visit with her parents so that's why we went to his place. Gayton was a good singer, as I said before, and Don had a guitar, so it was natural that he picked it up and started playing and singing. Every once in a while he would play a song that we all knew and we would join in with him. It was a great evening and I guess Don's house was the only one with a light on in the whole area, because it was three o'clock in the morning by now.

There was a knock on the door and Don answered, it was Jean, and she was upset and wondering what had been going on for so long and if I was okay. Of course it was time for me to go home as I should have been home 10 hours ago. I went straight to bed, and the young kids were up bright and early at 6 a.m., so you know who was going to change them and feed them and look after them. So with just less than three hours sleep, I had to do my duty. I fed, watered, changed and dressed them for outside. We took the wagon and walked into the woods. It was a beautiful morning and the sun was shining through the trees, and it was warm. We walked for a short distance, and then we all sat down and played around for a few minutes. I told the kids to play with the wagon and stay around me. I laid down on the heavy peat moss, which felt better than a mattress, and fell fast asleep. Two hours past, and I woke up with the birds still singing in the trees. It was one of the best sleeps that I had, for a long while. The kids were still there playing with the wagon. I laid there for a while, what seemed another couple of hours, just laying on the Moss and absorbing the sun.

We finally decided to go home and Jean and her mother thought that I would be complaining and really tired. That was such a good rest, that I was good for the rest of the day. After a short lashing that I had coming to me, everything was okay and that was my farewell to Goose from a couple of friends from work.

We did our "out routine" with Harold a few days later, and all of us took the new Vanguard aircraft that TCA had just purchased and had a nice flight to Montréal. Our stay there was only for a couple of days and we parted with Jean's mother, as she was going to do more visiting in eastern Canada. The rest of our trip home was by CN Railway and everyone enjoyed the trip home.

Coming out of Isolation – Going Home

Coming out of isolation is hard to describe to someone who hasn't experienced it. During that period, the children became two years older, and they have a lot of adjusting ahead, to the big city life. There were no traffic lights to be concerned with, nor were there many vehicles on the road, no sidewalks, and no noise of an artificial city. Fresh meats and vegetables and milk products were a treat. The sounds and smells of the big city are very noticeable. The hurrying and scurrying of people to catch a bus, or are in a hurry in their car to get home and eat, so that they can hurry out to some other appointment. This was a little scary at first, and it took a while to start driving in the flow of it all. They seemed to be in a hurry to get there, wherever that was. On the political scene, the Liberals had defeated the Conservatives and Canada had dumped the best aircraft ever built, THE ARROW. The Liberals were mad as heck at John D. and so moved the Air Force out of Saskatoon, leaving a NATO training base in Moose Jaw. For the next three years, the CFS and the UICP schools had no place to call home. They were scattered all over. For the next two years, the families of the air crews remained in the PM to use at the airport. Some of the wings were training at Winnipeg, some at Cold Lake and some at Portage la Prairie. The stations in Gimli and MacDonald were closed.

Winnipeg was too busy with commercial traffic to accommodate the Military, so one of the training officers would bring about six or eight DC3's and C45's to Saskatoon every Monday. There would be about six students in each aircraft, and they would go up mutual for about four hours flying circuits, leave the circuit every once in a while and changing seats with each other, until everyone had some training in. The crew would stay in a local hotel downtown until Friday. They would fuel up, do a few approaches and head for home and do the same the next week.

Saskatoon had the most sunshine days in all of Canada according to the meteorologists, and so it was a good place to get in lots of flying time (good weather flying). Our traffic dropped considerably, and most of the Military flying took place on Fridays and Mondays, these were the pilots without a place to call home, so they would commute back and forth to the various bases they had been assigned to.

Saskatoon's Staff was cut in half, some went to Ottawa, Regina and the bulk went to Winnipeg Center. This was the first time that Controllers were forced to move and some sort of system had to be devised, so that any time later if this came up again, the same system would have to be used in all fairness to everyone. Over the next few years, the Air Force side was dismantled, first the curling rink then some of the buildings. All the living quarters were sold to a real estate Consortium and they are still in use today. The north field became a graveyard for old aircraft, mostly old C119's and Neptune's, Harvard's and C45's. And later on the base was used as a crown assets disposal yard.

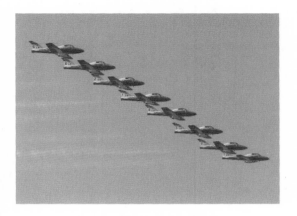

Canadian Snowbirds Moose Jaw

Ken Baskin Goose Bay

Marcotte Goose Bay

Sid Bower Goose Bay

Ken Baskin and Roy Cushway fishing Goose Bay

Fly Fishing Camp Goose Bay

Ritzy's Cabin

Roy Cushway – The Catch Goose Bay

Air Traffic Control
- Book 6

*The mind unlearns with difficulty, what
has long been impressed on it*

—Seneca

1958 - AN IMPORTANT TIME IN ATC.

The controller's lifestyle was different than your average Canadian. And that was another reason why they seemed to stick together. The shift work kept them away from the routines of their neighbors. The family had to get used to a different way of having meals and the whole household would rotate around a shift of the controller. Christmas and New Year's was probably the hardest on the wife and kids. Some Controllers were able to take leave and that was generally given to those with children, until the rebel group of new Controllers came on the scene around the middle of the 1960's. They declared discrimination against the single and unmarried controller. This was fair, I guess, as times were changing and so was the way we lived.

The traffic was generally light on Christmas Day and Boxing Day so there was no need to have a full staff on duty. But someone had to be there and from year to year or we used to share the work-load. If you worked Christmas you would have New Year's off, and vice versa usually. Many times I remember sitting down to Christmas dinner at noon with the families so that I could make it to work for the three o'clock shift. This shift work was especially hard on the wife who had to plan her household routine around my shift. The kids noticed that things around the house were different then than the neighbors. Today, it may be worse, or it may be better as quite a few have working lives, and then they both have a plan for day care, holidays and other appointments around a shift of the controller.

Ground Control Radar Installed

Soon after the Raytheon radar was installed in 1957, "those in the know" decided that due to the heavy training program of the Military at Saskatoon that GCA unit should be installed. This was the second unit to be installed in Canada. The first one was just completed and operational at Churchill, Manitoba.

Here then is a short explanation of its capabilities when installed at a station.

A new, low-cost and readily portable ground control approach unit, which enables aircraft to land safely under unfavorable conditions, began operating at Saskatoon RCAF station. Designated as quad radar, the new GCA equipment is the second unit of its kind in service in Canada. The first is at Fort Churchill, Manitoba, where the initial tests were carried out.

GCA enables an operator at Quad radar screen on the airfield to control an aircraft coming in to land by giving the pilot instructions over a two-way radio. The pilot need only watch his altimeter, compass and indicated airspeed dials and adjust his altitude, direction and airspeed according to the operator's instructions. The aircraft is seen by the operator as a moving dot and the runway as a lighted line on the face of the radar screen. Another line representing the path the aircraft must follow in approaching the runway runs diagonally across the screen, meeting the line at the touchdown point. GCA systems can bring an aircraft down to a specified point on the runway, under conditions of almost zero visibility, with perfect safety.

Quad radar combines into one unit, weighing less than a ton, the functions of four different radar systems. A search system is used for the initial recognition of aircraft coming within its scanning range and the guidance of the aircraft to the approach glide path. Once on that pass the precision approach system will show the altitude, range and bearing of the aircraft and its position in relation to the path line, following it to the final touchdown. A third system is used to direct the aircraft along a taxi strip once it has landed, and a fourth system, for height finding has a greater elevation range than the search system and its used for directing the landing approach of such aircraft as jets approaching from 50,000 feet, helicopters making near vertical landings and for providing elevation information to aircraft in the vicinity of the airfield.

The search and height finding equipment system can detect aircraft up to 50,000 feet within 40 miles. One radar screen serves all four systems. A touch of a switch changes both the functions of the equipment and the type of picture on the screen. Several features of Quad radar are new to GCA. Precision approach landings can be affected from any direction at the touch of a switch, unlike normal GCA equipment which can only give one picture from one direction. The operator and his equipment can be housed in the control tower or other protected spot up to 10,000 feet from the radar antenna, although not having the full capabilities of the heavier units (e.g. quad radar can direct only one aircraft at a time.)

The new unit will increase safety of flying operations at the Saskatoon airport. It will be available to civilian aircraft provided they have the proper radio frequencies. At present, the antenna and control unit are located at the intersection of the two main runways. However, later on permanent installation of the control unit will be made in the department of transport approach control unit on the second floor of the terminal building.

The air traffic control system worked in reverse to other working environments, or it when a new piece of equipment that was added to the systems, it nearly always required additional staff to operate it. Normally, additions of equipment would reduce the staff.

Most Controllers were very proud of the work that they did. In the early days when money was scarce and wearing apparel was usually a clean pair of pressed pants and a sports shirt. As time went on and things were looking up, dress code changed. A white shirt and tie with a suit or a pair of clean pressed dress pants were common. People wondered from their vantage point on the ground what a guy walking around the tower behind the tinted glass was really up to.

Simulator too late

Working with the new radar took a lot of our time and learning was a hands-on experience. About two years after the radar had been in operation, a simulator was installed. Since it cost lots of money those in the know wanted us to make use of it. As a learning aid it was useless, as far as we were concerned. We had already learned the hard way. Later on, when new Controllers came into the IFR part of the control system, then it was a good tool. It got them used to the Saskatoon area, the nav-aid's, traffic patterns and letdown procedures.

The information from the simulator was fed into a scope that the controller was using operationally. One to several targets could be simulated by one controller who acted as the pilot of all the aircraft he had put on the scope. The simulator was sitting on the left side of the arrival control console. To simulate a problem, a curtain was drawn between the two and the Controllers would holler at each other through the curtain. The system was not used very much because the controller was usually busy with real aircraft and didn't want to get caught mixing real targets with simulated ones. This did happen to one guy and scared the heck out of him, because he didn't know which were real and which were not. The day shift staffed three Controllers in the radar room. One was on departure control, one on arrival control, and one flight data coordinator. The controller on data was supposed to keep a written record of the traffic in the area, on strips of paper in plastic strip holders, in a four bay board. The board was set up with north to the top and the strip is laid out as close as possible to how the aircraft moved over the radar scope. He tried to keep the board up to date so that when things got hot and heavy traffic wise, the radar Controllers could glance over to the board, refresh his memory of all the traffic he was controlling and any that would be coming on the scene that he was not yet talking to.

One day when there was a lot of Military from Moose Jaw, Cold Lake and Saskatoon in the air, and the weather dropped at all the other stations except Saskatoon; there was a sudden a build up of traffic in the Saskatoon area. The Regina and Winnipeg airports had socked in also, so there was about eight diversions of civil aircraft from there, as well as our own schedule traffic.

Lorne was working flight data, Fred was working departure control, and I was on approach control. Lorne was getting traffic on the land-line faster than you could post it on the board, so he let us know that the board was not up to date. The wind was from the Northeast, so we were able to use the long east-west runway. As the traffic and the noise level built up, we made a mutual agreement to climb all the traffic east to 6,000 feet. Then if they wanted to go west or south west, put them on a heading out to 220° and change them over to me. I was able to keep the inbound traffic coming and we were able to use five-mile separation or 1,000 feet vertical. The traffic built up lasted for about two hours. When it was over, Lorne had to ask us what traffic went where, to bring his strips up to date. Management needed them for their monthly traffic count and statistics, otherwise we could have forgotten about that part of the operation.

The air force pilots always had a good sense of humor, and they often carried that with them at work as well as at play. When the radar was first on the air, we were getting in as much practice as possible.

The pilots were inventing new ways to test the system. To prove that the system was not too involved and I guess to impress on the Controllers that this stuff was good. It was a great aid in controlling, but don't believe everything that you see. Red Morris made the first point by flying into the cone of ambiguity. He then called for radar position report. The cone was the portion directly overhead the radar antenna and increased in width from the ground up. Sometimes the target would appear to be west of the station when in fact the aircraft was still overhead. It could be a difference of three or four miles. The controller was relying on raw radar targets. There were no transponders then, the only way that we could positively identify an aircraft was to give it a 45° turn, or identify it over a known fix that was marked on the overlay map of the radar.

There were lots of jets up flying around, that day at 1,000 on top, so to give the position report, it would be necessary to give him a turn. The controller gave him a turn for ident and waited to see the blip he thought would be Red making the turn. Another aircraft in the same area made a turn and the controller identified the wrong aircraft. Red made his point very effectively. Two other pilot instructors were up in a c45 one day and when they had finished doing their thing, they called radar for a vector to the runway. They gave their approximate position, heading and altitude. There was about a 60 knot wind from the East that day. The controller gave him 45° turn and identified the aircraft and began the vector. The aircraft was heading east into the wind and there are lots of the angels on the scope, angels are little dots on the radar that looked like aircraft, some the size of aircraft. The two guys in the C45 decided to slow down the aircraft as slow as they could without a stall. This made the target seem as though it was not moving sometimes and in fact, the blip moved backwards a few times. The controller now was uncertain that he may be looking at the wrong blip on the scope and so asked the aircraft to make another turn for identification. He got the aircraft going with the wind and finished the vector. The two pilots got quite a bang out of that. It was just another lesson to put in the back of the noggin for future use.

Some False Starts

A controller was getting traffic to an aircraft climbing out of Saskatoon, one day. It turned out to be a flock of those rare whooping cranes above the clouds about 8,000 feet. So as a controller became more experienced with the equipment that he was using, he always kept it in the back of his mind to not completely trust and I guess that is why when a controller is using his separation standards each and every day, he always throws in a mile or two extra for his wife and one for the kids and another for the mother-in-law.

I had an aircraft that was coming to Saskatoon from the North Country. It was flown by a bush pilot that very rarely came to the big city. Don't get me wrong, those guys were the backbone of the aviation industry and they were often called upon to fly in situations that no one should ever be subject to. They were the true seat-of-the-pants Fliers. They quite often fly IFR, but out of control airspace, and not by choice. This pilot was coming from the west and identified about 30 miles west of the station, at 6,000 feet. A clearance to him was "cleared to the Saskatoon beacon direct maintain 6,000 feet no delay expected." A scheduled airliner was just climbing out westbound identified on radar and leaving 2,000 feet. The two aircraft were about to pass so close to the field that the easiest solution was to hold the North Star down to 4,000 feet until they passed. A controller has a sixth sense, and I have seen it displayed many times over the years.

This particular time I climbed the North Star well clear of the inbound, even though it should not have been necessary. As they passed 3,000 feet, and the light aircraft inbound reported out of 3,000 feet descending, my heart missed a beat or two. I guess it's the consequences that would have come, that scare the guy after the fact. Those are the things that he has to shake off when off-duty, so that he doesn't replay them in his mind and come back the next day exhausted before he has done any work.

There was a controller involved in an aircraft accident that was not even his fault and he had to take some time off work. He used to have nightmares, often wake up in the middle of the night and be talking to the pilot that had died in a fatal air crash, trying to change something so that the accident wouldn't happen. He was under the care of a doctor for a few months, and thought he could go back to work. The first day at the workplace just send him back to those days, he had to go home never to control again.

1958 Important Time in ATC

The year 1958 is an important year for the Air Traffic Controller. The number of aircraft using the service had increased. The number of personnel had quadrupled. Winnipeg had grown from the squatty little shack lost somewhere along the old Military hangar line. Bits and pieces had been added to it and the number of Controllers had grown to more than 90 in the Center alone. The number of Controllers at Saskatoon had grown to 25. Air traffic control was always behind any growth by at least five years, and any move to improvement would take at least five more years to implement. The Controllers in Winnipeg were becoming rest-less with the slowness of the bureaucracy, and a small group had gotten together and decided to organize the Controllers all across Canada. Letters went out to all the units to get the response from the Controllers. The response was overwhelming, and the meeting was arranged in Winnipeg by Don Mortin, a Winnipeg Center controller. At least two representatives from Saskatoon were to attend, to go through the painful procedure of setting up the constitution and the objectives of the association. Lorne Billingsley and I were elected to go as representatives for the Saskatoon Tower and terminal unit.

Dues were paid on a voluntary basis and the money collected was used for material and expenses for meeting rooms and things associated with the first meeting. The delegates received an allowance of $10 per day to cover hotel and meals and any other expense. This of course was not near enough and the Controllers paid the rest out of their own pocket. It was the responsibility of each controller to find his own way to Winnipeg. Lorne and I had enquired through the Air Force, if it would be possible to bum a ride with any aircraft going that way. Controllers were able to get the odd ride, if they were willing to wait long hours for a plane to come that was going the right way, and had room on board.

The Flight Control Officers said "no sweat"; we could go on the first flight plane that was going east, when we're ready to go. We just had to sit in the waiting room in the Air Force flight planning room and catch the first empty aircraft. We had only been waiting about an hour or so and we were advised that a DC3 was coming from Edmonton en route to Winnipeg. We only had a small bag of belongings, and we're able to carry them on board. After takeoff, and when the aircraft was level at 5,000 feet, the first officer came to the passenger compartment. We were the only ones on the aircraft besides the crew. He asked us if we would like a soft drink, and handed us a piece of paper with a position report on it and are estimated ramp time at Winnipeg. We thought this was unusual for the Air Force to be going through all this trouble for a couple of lowly Controllers bumming a ride. He came back from the cockpit several times during the course of the trip to chat and give us more information and to be sure that we were comfortable. We had a box lunch on the trip and thoroughly enjoyed ourselves.

The noise level on the DC3 was high by today's standards, but we endured the ride. Nearing Winnipeg, he came back again and asked who he should bill for the trip. We were dumbfounded, we didn't know what to say because this was the first time the question had ever come up. It turned out that this particular aircraft was a scheduled run that the Air Force flew between Edmonton and Winnipeg. Even the flying Officer in Saskatoon didn't know that we would be charged for the ride. Since Lorne and I didn't have the money to pay him, he said he would charge the Department of Transport. We still thought that he was pulling our leg and we went along with the gag.

During the course of the next few days in Winnipeg, we let it be known to those in the know that the Department was going to be charged for our ride from Saskatoon. They all laughed and we laughed with them. The next day, Vic Skinner (Chief of Winnipeg Center) made a few inquiries, and that evening informed the meeting that no Controllers are to bum rides with the Air Force without the Department authorization. If you did, you would be on your own and the Department would not be responsible.

The meetings for the next few days were very long. We scrounged a few meals, and made it home again, with a few dollars that we had in our pockets. The Toronto Controllers were the most disagreeable group at the convention. The whole meeting was about to break-up on several issues but the rest of the Controllers had come to an agreement. The Toronto group went away angry, and would not join as things stood. With some persuasion, a few months later, they agreed to come into the group.

That was the beginning of the Canadian Air Traffic Controllers Association (CATCA). From that time on, working conditions and salaries improved, and anyone who had never known who or what an Air Traffic Controller was, would find out in the years to come. The Government were becoming impatient with their continuing strikes during the various holiday seasons. Times changed, demands changed, and hard-nosed bargaining was in. There would be several issues appear on the negotiating table, but the one that causes the most controversy was a bilingual issue and it lasted a few years with a lot of hard feelings between Controllers, Management, and the Government.

With the growth of the Regional Office and the Training School, many positions were created and the opportunity for advancement or a chance to get out of active control was available. Our first long stay in Winnipeg came about in 1958. Five Controllers in Saskatoon qualified to attend the IFR school. One instructor was Murray Sutherland, a Winnipeg tower controller. Later he became Chief of the tower. The other was Bob Turner, a Winnipeg Center controller, later to become Western Regional Manager in Edmonton. There were thirteen Controllers and two instructors for the three month course. It was the first one of its kind, so we had to feel our way through, so to speak. The expenses allowed were $100 per month to cover everything. Some stayed at the YMCA downtown, some stayed with friends, and two of us stayed in a private home where we had board and room supplied. We brown bagged it every day, had a good breakfast and supper with our hosts and amazingly, we stayed within the budget allowed.

Air Traffic Control
   - Book 7

SASKATOON - MILNER RIDGE

> *Our bravest and best lessons are not learned through success, but through misadventure.*

> —A.B.Alcott

The Decompression Chamber

One year when everything around ATC was going pretty good, someone "in the know" decided that all Controllers should go through the decompression chamber on the Air Force side, and take a ride in one of the T-birds to better understand the pilot's problem. It was not that the pilot really had a problem, but for the controller to see the inside "up close workings" of an aircraft that we were dealing with from day to day. They would call this the familiarization flight. I was the only one not in favor of this procedure because of the danger of ending my career with a blown eardrum, and besides, I think that the rapport between the pilot and controller at the time was good. The Controllers were (pardon the pun) under pressure to go to the chamber, and take the test and get a card endorsed for Military jet rides.

Several Controllers had taken the test and things were going good, until one of them had a problem with the rapid decompression part of the test. The simulator would take the chamber to an altitude of 25,000 feet, and do a slow descent to ground level, and then after being subjected to several minutes at altitude, doing math tests and simple problems, he again would go through a decompression explosion to simulate loss of pressurization at altitude. This part of the test was the most dangerous because the eardrum could become permanently damaged, or on a rapid decompression, his ears would not clear and the chamber would have to be compressed to altitude again and slowly brought back to ground level. If this was to happen to the controller in a bad weather situation in a real aircraft, the pilot may not be able to take it up again and risk not having enough fuel or not being able to make another approach at that airport.

Damaged ear drum

For the pilot this was a compulsory part of his training because he was working in this type of environment every day, but the controller was not. One controller came back from the test with a damaged eardrum and the tests stopped for Controllers immediately. "Those in the know" decided that they didn't want to be held responsible for ending a good controller's career. Two examples of how this prevailed was a report from two Controllers after a check-ride in the aircraft. The usual route to go was on a trip to Winnipeg, about an hour's flight time, do jet letdowns, land, refuel, visit the Centre, climb back in the T-bird and return to Saskatoon, to do a jet letdown and shoot a few circuits with some close patterns thrown in. This was just in case the controller hadn't gotten sick yet.

The first controller reported that he got sick, soon after departure from Saskatoon, honked all the way to Winnipeg in the helmet that they had given him to wear. He didn't see anything from above the clouds and the instrument panel was moving in a clockwise rotation and he didn't see anything there either. The whole trip was a loss of half a day for him and the other half was spent at home recovering. That was the first and last trip he ever took in a T-bird. The pilot had loaned the flying suit to a controller, and it was a smelly mess when he returned it so that controller figured that he had gotten even with him for making him sick. The other controller was more fortunate he made the trip to Winnipeg and back. "No sweat" as they would say. The pilot couldn't let him off that easy, so he requested a series of close patterns in the circuit until the controller's stomach was coming out of his mouth. The only thing that the controller learned from the FAM trip was not to go again.

Fishing on Falcon Lake, Manitoba

So the pressure was off anyone from then on, if they didn't want to take the decompression test then so be it. We could still take rides with the Air Force as they had room and we were invited. Since we knew most of the crew on the other side, they always were more than happy to take you wherever they happen to be going. Jim Conway had a cabin on Falcon Lake East of Winnipeg. We were working the same shift with the same days off, so he suggested that we go to the cabin for a couple of days. We bummed a ride on B25 going to Winnipeg. This aircraft was a bomber trainer and was built for the crew up front and a couple of gunners in the back. The only way to get from the cockpit to the rear, when airborne was to climb through a small space above the Bombay to the rear compartment. There was no luxury on this aircraft. In the rear, where we sat most of the time, the noise level was so high we couldn't talk to each other. The droning of the two engines, right outside from where we sat was enough to make a head spin.

Hard on the ears

As it turned out, the crew would be in Winnipeg the same length of time as us, so we had a guaranteed ride back home. The weather was good and we had a relaxing couple of days swimming, water skiing, and our first time sailing. The sailing part was a disaster but the bug had bitten and in the years to come would occupy quite a bit of our leisure time. We had a few drinks the night before coming home and it was a mistake. The noise and droning of the B25 for a couple of hours was almost enough to drive a preacher to drink.

Refreshers

Each Region adopted its own system of training and retraining, called refresher courses. They were usually held from October to February. As far as Winnipeg was concerned each unit would send one controller to make up a class for a week. We were generally told which hotels were allowed to stay in. The first hotel (The Marlborough Hotel) that we stayed in had an expensive part and not so expensive part for Federal Government Employees.

These rooms were generally with a shared bathroom. I was there for about three days when the controller from Regina came to my door and asked if I would unlock my side of the door so that he could use the bathroom. I don't know what he was doing for washing and shaving, let alone using the toilet until then. The sheets on the bed where white cotton, well starched, and the first night just about scared the daylights out of me. The air in the hotel was super dry and when you turned off the lights to go to bed, the movement of your body over the sheets would produce a great display of fire, like St. Elmo's fire that occurred on the wings of some aircraft caused by the static electricity in the room.

Some tricks Moe did

After one of the refresher trips to the Air Force side of the field at Winnipeg airport we were invited to the mess for a couple before we went home for supper. Moe Sutherland was giving a couple of us a ride home in his car, and somewhere along a deserted road he stopped the car. Bob and I were in the back seat and wondered why he had stopped. Moe turned around in his seat and asked

Bob to push a little button near the top of the window on the back of the car. So Bob reached over and pushed it. Moe said that's fine, and started driving again. We didn't want to ask him outright, what the problem was and what Bob had done to fix it. Bob thought he had done something but didn't know what. Of course Moe was pulling our leg and it bothered Bob all that night. Next day Moe had a grin on his face a mile long and Bob knew he had been had.

Trip to Milner Ridge

Controllers were always pulling tricks on each other. When we were on an IFR training course, Moe Sutherland and then Bob Turner were the instructors for our class, and they wanted to arrange a tour of the American radar site at Milner Ridge near Beausejour Manitoba. This radar site at Milner Ridge was part of the mid-Canada line and had the codename of BOXFILE (this was an American Military base). I had worked there before when I lived in Winnipeg, and belonged to the Reserve Fighter Control Operators of the RCAF. The two weeks training put me through all the positions of the site that were occupied by the control operators. The big clear plastic control board covered the whole of North America and plotters stood behind the plastic, and plotted positions of aircraft movements transmitted to them from the control officers positions.

The instructors thought that because we were obliged to give AMIS (air movement information service) information to this site when requested, a better understanding of the operation would be of benefit to us so we spent half a day there. At about four o'clock in the afternoon we were ready to drive back home. The officer in charge invited us to the Mess for one for the road which turned out to be several for some Controllers. Since we would only be there a short time someone suggested that we play the numbers game to determine who would buy the drinks. I have forgotten how it works now, but the guy who ended up with the wrong number was the winner (or loser) and paid for a round. Sid Bower got stuck and paid for 15 drinks that were only about two bits (25¢) per drink so didn't break him. He wanted to recoup his losses and called for another game. He lost three more times and we declared that he shouldn't have to pay any more. There was lots of laughing, joking, and everyone feeling no pain; we decided we better get home.

Vote for Marty

About half an hour after leaving BOXFILE, everyone had to go to the washroom, so when we hit the town of Beausejour we stopped at a local pub for a beer and went to the washroom. There was an election going on in the Province at the time and there were many posters around outside the pub advertising different political parties. Marty spotted the one for the Social Credit candidate and immediately declared himself the campaign Manager for this man. This pub is normally busy if they had two people in it at any one time, so when we arrived the owner was dumbfounded by the new found business all of a sudden.

The place came alive and the tables were filled with glasses of beer. Marty jumped up on one of the empty tables pulled a long letter (from his wife) out of his pocket and pretended to read his campaign speech. It was terrific and I think the bartender and the other locals in the pub where thoroughly convinced that they should vote for this guy. We will never know for sure. We arrived back in Winnipeg all in good health and vowed never to do that again.

You Work Alone

At home in Saskatoon again, our station was the alternate airport for Cold Lake, Alberta Military Base. The pilots from there flying F104's at the time would come to Saskatoon for a practice approach and overshoot, returning to Cold Lake. Some nights, 10 of them would come about two minutes apart. These things move fast and the whole operation would be over within a half an hour. Controllers on the evening shift were expected to work alone, that is they would be the only person on duty for the eight hour shift. They would be expected to go to the washroom down the hall when traffic permitted, not when you had to go. Eating on the job was a way of life. Operating the three positions would involve combining the two radar positions to one, and if anything would suffer it had to be the coordinating position.

Some Early Stories

The controller had three hats to wear on the evening and midnight shift and he got tired of calling himself a different name each time he changed his duty, so the term Saskatoon Terminal eventually was adopted. The F104's were very cooperative to us and knew that there was only one man on duty, so when we asked for an altitude report after they completed the approach, and were on their way back to Cold Lake, they would do a climb straight up to the altitude. By the time the controller had said the words report level at 25,000 the pilot would come back with level and then he could proceed with no further restrictions. The pilots that did a lot of flying in and out of Saskatoon were very considerate of the control problems and would bend over backwards to help a guy out of a tight situation. The controller got to know the pilots on the civil aircraft as well as the Military just by their voice. Sometimes we knew them by name, but many of the pilots that I worked with over the years were just voices on the radio, and blips on the radar. A lot of them I would never meet in person.

Central Experimental and Proving Establishment (CEPE)

The winter of 1958 was the warmest in history for Saskatoon. Some think the reason was because the Military decided to move their cold weather test facility from Cold Lake to Saskatoon. It was called Central Experimental and Proving Establishment (CEPE). There were several different types of aircraft under cold weather tests for that winter. Some of them were a couple of F86's, a couple of T33's, a Blackburn Beverley from Great Britain, a Vampire and several other smaller piston and jet aircraft. The pilots working on the tests had a radio set up in the hangar, which was hooked up to a recorder. They called it "wee radio". This was used in the tests as the pilot went through the routines he would run an open mic and just keep talking on this discreet frequency, reading off numbers and any other information that they were interested in. They would land, pick up the tape, and then do a debriefing on the operation.

Over the next few years, we became familiar with various new aircraft that were coming on line at a rapid pace. B -36,B- 47, B-52,C130, C133, KC 97, KC 135,C141 (Star lifter), C5 (Galaxy), CF 102 as well as many smaller civilian training aircraft and some executive jets.

Air Traffic Control
- Book 8

More Pilot and Controller stories

Sometime later, at the Officers Mess on a (tufor's) Friday there was a chance for Joel to get me, but he would also get a few others in the process. There was a serious game of shuffleboard going on between the CO and another officer. All Controllers and flyers in the mess were crowded around the board to watch the final shot that would decide the winner of the game. There was strict silence as the CO was going to make his shot. Then Joel did it, he released silent flatulence, which immediately cleared the mess and the outcome of the game was never determined. As a matter of fact, there was a bingo game the next night and the bartender said that they hadn't been able to clear the air out of the room yet.

Kjell (pronounced shell) was a controller who made the strong Swedish coffee. He was one of about seven or eight Controllers who lived in a house on Dufferin Street, each with a completely different personality and habits. But they all got along well, and the fact that they worked shift-work, the house never seemed crowded. It got the name of "house of ill repute" but that was only because they were all single young fellows and the odd girl would drop by for some socializing and good fun with some laughs. There seemed to be lots of that around there.

There was an American Air Force C 97 coming into Saskatoon to take on some fuel on his trip to Alert, Northwest Territories and he said he had room for anyone wanting a ride. Kjell decided he would take the trip and see some of the North Country. He came out to the airport and got on the aircraft and never saw the ground again until they touched down at Alert. It was -40° Fahrenheit and a blizzard in progress. They unloaded the cargo and took off again. He was gone about 24 hours and hadn't seen a thing.

Roger was a sharp controller who also lived in a house on Dufferin and he had a close friendship with one of the instructors from UICP School. In fact he had been up on rides in the T-birds with him. One day we had a visit from the Deputy Minister of Transport from Ottawa, carrying one of those big brown satchels that all people from Government carry when on a trip in the field. We were all curious as to why this man had come all the way out to little old Saskatoon. No one ever came out here from the big city without it being really important. We were working the day shift and when the shift changed Roger stayed behind. We all went to the house on Dufferin to find out what it was all about. When Roger came home he said that they had given him a choice to quit or resign. He said he wanted to go back to school and finish his career in education so he resigned. They had shown him a file that the RCMP had been keeping on him. Roger had the misfortune of growing up in the wrong era, because today it would not be tolerated. He had been a youth member of the CCF and a strong socialist; in fact he had room and boarded with Joe Phelps earlier and probably got a good indoctrination into socialism from him. Any meeting that he had attended was documented and then they said that due to the nature of his work it was considered a sensitive area and they would give him a job in another area other than air traffic control. What really didn't make sense was Roger completed his teaching training and was offered a job at Resolute Bay teaching the native school there. Resolute Bay was an American base for KC 97 and other Military aircraft, and Moscow Molly used to say on her broadcast that they kept an eye on the base and the new aircraft whenever the Americans move cargo or aircraft. Not that they would be getting their information from Roger but that it was considered a more sensitive place than Saskatoon ever was.

The Invisable U2

The U2 aircraft used to be in the air every day and we could hear them talking to their control base somewhere in the U.S., also we could see them go by on a clear day but they were so high they were hard to identify and besides no one really knew what kind of aircraft it was at that time. One day a U2 had engine problems north of Prince Albert, Saskatchewan, and had to land on the ice. Very soon a C-130 Hercules from the U.S. was dispatched with another engine and a ground crew of mechanics. They installed the new engine and the aircraft took off from the ice and headed south. That trip we had a good look at it as it went by. Soon after, the Russians also got a good look at it when they downed Gary Powers and the U2 aircraft over their soil on a spy mission.

The Lockheed Lightening

There was a controller with the initials SP and we all called him Sweet Pea. One Sunday morning he was working the tower and Ted and I were working the radar. There was an unwritten rule around that we would not use runway 14 for takeoffs if another runway could be used and especially early in the morning. If the wind was more than 10 mph and aircraft asked for it he got it. The wind was calm to five. The Lockheed Lightning's had come in the day before and were parked on the ramp down by the Air Force hangers. They are noisy airplanes. The squawk box between the tower and the terminal was open. It was built that way for some reason; I think cost was a factor. The tower controller just had to yell from a distance from the box with departure or whatever and we could hear it okay down below when it was quiet, we could also hear the conversation in the tower. The first lightning called for a taxi instructions and SP gave him runway 14. We heard that and pressed the button on the squawk box and said "you'll be sorry". SP said "the wind was 5 mph and he had to use it."

So the first Lightning took off with a noisy departure. We got on the phone and muffled our voice and complained violently the way we sometimes have gotten calls from the city folk before. We also engaged the services of the radio operator to phone and complain and we could hear SB calmly and quietly explaining why he had to use the runway. The next one called and he also was given runway 14. We called upstairs again and said "you'll be sorry". He didn't know that we had heard him on the phone or that it was us that were phoning him. The other one took off in a great burst of noise, so we got on the phone again and complained several times. Each time we could hear SB calmly explaining the noise. Finally the other one called for taxi and SP said "you have to use runway 26, we're getting too many complaints from the city folk about the noise at this time of the morning". The Lightning's were a noisy airplane that's for sure, and they sounded like two Mustangs in formation full-out.

F86 Crash on Final

A crash happened one day around 10 o'clock in the morning. One of the UICP instructors was up on a routine exercise and had just completed a letdown and was on the GCA portion of his final run for a full stop landing. The F86 was about 8 miles on final for runway 32, which would bring him directly over the city from the southeast. The GCA controller was just getting ready to give him his steady spiel for the talk down and the blip disappeared from the radar. The F86 had flamed out and went into a farmer's yard, just missed a house and ended up beside the barn. The pilot survived but had hurt his back pretty bad which put him out of flying for the rest of his life. This immediately brought up the concern of aircraft approaching the airport from the southeast and flying over the city. It didn't seem to bother those that make the decisions though, because the airport is filled with houses around the south end of the airport, and with an industrial park on the East side, right under the approach path of the long east west runway.

The Pilots Teaching the Controllers a Thing or Two

The Controllers had a good rapport with the pilots on the station and any problems that would arise were solved amiably. A few of the flying officers that I can remember were Doc Payne, Red Morris, Mouse Reynolds, and Jock Abbott. There were more of these fine fellows and we had a close relationship with them in the curling rinks and on the baseball diamonds, in the bar and at the barbecues.

Mouse was a hot rod of the Air force, he liked to fly the T-birds wide open, close to the ground and do fancy spins and things with the aircraft.

One fine day I was working the control position in the tower and it was getting close to noon and all the aircraft would be coming in for a couple of circuits before they went in for dinner. Mouse called about 10 miles west and asked for a low pass from west to east. This type of procedure was a no-no for us as well as for them. Unless they wanted us to check if their gear was down and clean underneath, or if they had just completed the range approach and were on an overshoot. I approved the low pass down the runway as there was no traffic near the field at the time, so good old Mouse came barreling across the horizon. He was so close to the ground that he was making the dust stir in the fields to the west, he crossed the field below the windsock in the middle of the field which was about 25 feet high. He passed below the tower that was 75 feet down the Air Force ramp, and back up into the wild blue yonder. I knew we were in trouble when I spotted him coming over the horizon, but it was too late to change anything. It took less than a minute and it was all over.

The phone started ringing immediately, and it was the CO wanting to know what the heck was going on over there and who was in the T-bird. I thought that I would be a good buddy and said "it was Mouse and he was doing a low approach and over-shoot off a range approach". I got my ears burned. When Mouse landed and was taxiing I let him know that the CO was upset and wanted to see him in his office soon as he got in. I told Mouse what I had told him about low approach off of a practice range approach. Mouse went into the CO office and said that he already knew what he wanted because the tower had warned him about how mad the CO was and he said he wasn't on a range approach, but on a low pass approved by the tower. I guess Mouse didn't get in much trouble over that because he was out flying in the afternoon. But the "fit hit the shan" for me and everybody was on my back for what I had done. So the lesson has been learned early in my career never approve a low pass, no matter what, only if the request was accompanied by the word "emergency".

"Great men are very apt to have great faults; and the faults appear greater by their contrast with their Excellencies."

—C. Simmons.

There was one pilot from the UICP School who was a cut above the rest and he let everyone know it. That is everything he did or said was flawless, and he expected the same from everyone else, or you heard about it. He was known as the EAP (exceptional in all phases). In later years he would leave the Air Force and commenced a career for an airline and one bad weather day he attempted a landing in Regina when conditions dictated that it should not have been attempted. The DC-9 slid off the runway and a lot of damage occurred to the airplane. He immediately began to blame everyone from the meteorology staff, to the airport manager, to the firefighting crews, to a controller for the predicament that he found himself in.

This is My Story and I'm Sticking to It

Runway 0826 had been extended to 8,300 feet and resurfaced; it was considered one of the smoothest runways in Canada. The radar had been installed and was operational but would not be commissioned until 1958. We were told to use the radar and get used to it and keep track of the number of practice runs that we did. This was to be done in VFR weather conditions and was to be requested by the pilots; although we could solicit it, if it was done discreetly. We discreetly conned various aircraft into practicing an approach with us to rack up our totals and hone our vectoring techniques. When the GCA unit was installed it was easier to get the runs because GCA approaches were part of the Air Force training, and we would start the vector from 15 or 20 miles out and then the GCA controller would not have to change the set up of his quad radar and we would hand the aircraft off to the GCA unit at 3 miles on final.

I had logged over 200 runs by Nov. 6th, 1958 according to the log sheet that I had ripped out of the log book before it was destroyed. Most of the Controllers were very efficient with the use of the scope and radar being new, the resolution was superb. We could see almost anything and could distinguish cars and trucks on the highway, trains on the tracks and even aircraft taxiing to and from the hangar line. When we gave traffic to an aircraft that we were vectoring it would include something like this. "Check traffic, C 45, 11:30, 5 miles altitude unknown". It was always given in the same order and it included aircraft type, position of the traffic relative to his, using the clock method, a distance from him in miles and the altitude if known. There was a train that used to run from Saskatoon to Prince Albert and another that we could see about 25 miles southwest of the station. We could set the clock with them except in the winter.

Anyway a favorite saying for the controller when vectoring an aircraft in either of these areas was to give traffic as "check traffic

12 o'clock 5 miles on track" and aircraft would come back "check train on track".

My Emergency with a piece of Non-Commissioned Equipment – 1958

November 17, 1958 was logged in our logbook as a requirement of the system for using the radar under emergency conditions. It was always hard for a controller to get a pilot to declare an emergency because they felt that it wasn't an emergency until all possible actions had been tried and there wasn't any place else to go but down. Some didn't have time to declare an emergency because they were already coping with one. They used to think that they had to be on fire and in grave danger before they would declare. There was an emergency frequency, 121. 5 MHz that was always kept open for emergency purposes, but some radio operators and Controllers got so tied up in emergency saying that they didn't want to tie up the frequency in case someone else had an emergency and wanted to use it. Our radar was not commissioned for use yet, and was only to be used in emergencies.

This emergency started out like all others, just a routine situation. A T33 was on a flight from Vancouver to Gimli Manitoba and was in the vicinity of Regina Saskatchewan at 30,000 feet when he was told that the Gimli weather was WOXOF pronounced WOCKSOFF which meant the weather was "indefinite ceiling zero sky obscured visibility zero in fog". The pilot called Saskatoon terminal, because we were the alternate on his flight plan. The time was about 6:30 p.m. in the evening. Saskatoon weather was 800 overcast visibility 12 miles, just within limits for a range approach. The T-bird was estimated to arrive at 6:50 so after the necessary coordination was done I advised the tower controller of the diversion to our station. I was working the terminal unit alone, as we often did on the evening shift, and there was one controller in the tower. There was a VFR specialist from Winnipeg visiting in the tower, a young boyish looking kid, who had a lot on the ball, and that is why he had advanced to the position he was in so quickly. But his over eager reflexes would play an important part in this story later on. With the wind calm the best runway to use was 08. It was the longest and the aircraft could come straight in off the range approach. Also the minimum altitudes were the lowest in that quadrant.

As the T-bird started his approach the weather office called with a special observation of measured ceiling 200 feet overcast visibility 12 miles. This was related to the pilot and he asked for high intensity lights. Runway 08 had high intensity runway and approach lights and would normally be set on strength three unless requested higher by the pilot. There were five settings of strength from one to five. Tower had the lights on five and this would help the pilot see the runway through the cloud as his minimum on approach was to be 500 feet. If he couldn't see anything, he was to overshoot and try again or go to an alternate. But he had already committed himself to this airport and had started the approach, which meant he would not have enough fuel to divert to Cold Lake which was his closest alternate from here.

I had told him the situation with our radar and that the best that I could do was to monitor his approach and give him position and distance information. We had practiced ppi approaches (planned position indicator), which was doing a vector to touchdown giving distance and as much information but no altitude, only the altitude that he should be every half-mile from the end of the runway. I had the "patter" down pat as they would say in the business and I was confident in doing that type of approach if I had to. He had completed the letdown from 25,000 feet and was on final approach doing very good and he had the lights in sight at 3 miles. I called up to the tower on the hot-line and gave the position as 3 miles. The fellow from Winnipeg with the quick reflexes reached over to the light panel in the tower and turned the strength down to three, which she had no right to do without permission. The pilot let out a yell and said "whoooa somebody turned my lights out", and he had to overshoot.

The second approach was done from 4,000 feet, and with the distance information that I had been giving him and suggested headings he was on final again very shortly, but the weather had changed to a ceiling of 150 feet and 12 miles forward visibility. He saw the light's okay but was over the threshold before he got a good look, and he said he thought he could make it if he made another approach. So I offered my services, if he would accept them as this was becoming an emergency. Declaring emergency meant reams of paperwork for the pilot and for the controller and if anything was to go wrong an investigation which, no one ever wanted to go through.

I started the vector from his overshoot position east of the field and brought him around close to the field and the turn onto final at 5 miles from the end of the runway. I had informed the tower, what I was doing and under no circumstances to touch the field lighting until the airplane was on the ground. The radar was so darn good I was able to put him on the center line and give distance and altitudes that he should be at every half-mile to touch-down. I advised him that he was over the threshold and to take over. There was long silence and we could not hear the usual roar that a T-bird made if he had overshot the runway, so we sat in silence for what seemed an eternity waiting for something from the pilot on the frequency.

He finally said he was on the ground and turned on the taxiways toward the hangar line, and he ran out of gas. The engine shut down and he had to be towed to the hangar line. He had dirty drawers I think, and I didn't feel too well myself. He phoned me later from the Officer's Mess and invited me over for a few drinks and thanked me from the bottom of his heart for the help. I had to refuse the invitation because I was on a quick change shift, from evenings, to day shift and would have to be in at 7 a.m. The reported weather on landing was ceiling 100 feet overcast visibility 10 miles. My log says that ironically I did not check out as a qualified Radar approach controller until January 5, 1959. The pay for an approach controller then was $427.50 per month gross.

Here's a thought for today: "Babblers, they always talk who never think"

A Grade 3 Air Traffic Controller was earning a salary of $4,300 to $4,700 per annum depending on how many years he had been at that position. Later on, in 1966, the controller would be hired on at $475 a month while training with up to four months training in a control tower at $300 a month and if he/she checked out and had the license endorsed a salary of $382 a month, with promotion opportunities within the system to $731 a month.

Winnipeg Convention 1950 Roy in Middle

Roy Cushway Saskatoon Terminal 1960

Refresher Course Winnipeg 1964

ATC Controllers Convention 1955

**(IFR SCHOOL - Winnipeg January 1958
Back Row: Left to right:**

**Jack Brown, Tom Hayes, Lorne Billingsley, Bill Jeshewski,
Lyle Davidson, Glen Mead, Roy Cushway**

Front Row: Left to Right

**Hank Batt, Marty Steiger, John Datskiw, Bob Turner, Murray
Sutherland, Bob Power, Bruce McEwen, Sid Bower)**

Air Traffic Control
   - Book 9

"Make 'em laugh; make'em cry; make'em wait."
—Charles Reade

Some old stories

The Saskatoon unit was considered small compared to the control centres across Canada. There were advantages to working at a smaller unit though, morale was high, great co-operation between the Chief of the unit and the Controllers.

The Controllers were closer to each other, because most outsiders really didn't understand their work or their abnormal 9-to-5 work routine. With shift work as a normal way of life for the controller, he rarely saw his neighbors and when he did, they would wonder if he ever went to work, because they would never see him.

When on evening or midnight shifts, with most units using the quick shift change, they would be off three days in a row and if he combined a couple of days of leave, then he would be off for a week. The Controllers were always "talking shop" when not at work and since the profession was rarely known or understood by the general public people tended to shy away. Controllers that worked together and got along with each other soon became personal friends and tended to stick together when not at work.

I had many friends during my career and I would hate to try to list them here for fear of missing some of them. Some sayings or mannerisms of these Controllers stand out and I can recall them because they have been rehashed so many times and they stick in my mind.

Just a couple more stories about my good friend Joel

Controllers would often stop at the KG Hotel on the way home for a couple, and talk over some of the events of the day. One day we were sitting at a table with a few drafts on the table and another controller named Moose walked in and sat down. It was a cold winter day about -30° Fahrenheit and no one wanted to stay too long as the car would get cold and besides Moose had just bought some fresh fruit, veggies and milk, so he didn't want to let them freeze in the car. He had just sat at the table and laid his keys and some money on the table to buy a round. Joel was in the process of telling a story and he was flailing his arms and hands around while explaining things. He would put his hands on the table now and then to explain something and in the process picked up the car keys to use to draw an invisible picture on the top of the table.

When he was finished or sometime during his explanation he slipped the keys in his pocket. He probably never noticed and may have thought they were his own in the hilarity of his explanation. Joel and I finished a couple of slurps that were left in our glasses, put on our coats and said farewell to Moose and the other Controllers at the table. I had just gotten home when the phone began ringing. It was Moose and he was mad as heck, and after he calmed down, I had to explain to him that I didn't have his car keys. But he said "you have them I saw you pick them up." I tried to console poor old Moose and suggested that it may have been

Joel, who had them. Over an hour had gone by, and the groceries in his car were probably near freezing point. Moose was unable to contact Joel because he had not gone straight home. Moose finally called a locksmith and the car door was opened in less than two minutes at a cost of $10.

The only good thing that came of the episode, for me at least was a lesson, and the next day I went to the corner hardware store and cut a couple of extra keys for the car.

One other day, the Controllers on the day shift had made arrangements to meet at the Senator hotel for a couple of draft. Joel was with us. After we had been there for a couple of hours we all got up to head for home. Soon after I got home the phone rang. It was Joel. He was fighting mad, and he accused me of hiding his car on him, and if I didn't tell them where it was he would phone the police. I had sympathy for Joel but couldn't help him in his problem. Joel either walked home or took the bus and then phoned the police. He told them he had parked the car behind the Senator and someone had stolen it. The police found his car about an hour or so later parked on 4th Ave about three blocks from the Senator, right where Joel had parked it. We had a lot of laughs over that one.

How to Tell It Was Close to Pay Day

The salary that we were getting at the time was not high by any means, but it was a living and the work was great. We had a small pot of money at work that the Controllers could borrow from when they were out of money, usually just before payday. We all used it now and then and some used it more than others. Also you could tell by a guy's lunch, how close it was to payday. We would look at each others' lunch and trade the odd sandwich. A sandwich in one hand and a mic in the other was a way of life for the controller.

One day Joel offered me a cold sliced cooked potato made into a sandwich with salt and lots of pepper on it between two slices of homemade bread. I declined the offer because I had never tasted cold potato sandwiches before; as a matter of fact I had never heard of them. When he first said that he had them, we all thought that he was joking, but that was what you did, when getting near to payday. It was some years later that a railway engineer friend of mine was making a joke about how poor he was, and that he would have to start eating potato sandwiches.

By comparison to the salaries at the time, about a 10 year gap, I guess you could consider us poor.

Beautiful Cold Winters

On those cold, cold mornings of winter with a high pressure ridge stuck over the prairies for a week or so, life would go on as usual and the jet jocks would go up and when they found out the conditions were ripe for leaving a contrail, they would go up to about 25,000 feet and fly under the rules of 1,000 on top, which meant VFR, at least 1,000 feet above all cloud, 10 or 20 of them would get up there and the controller didn't have to separate them or watch them until they were ready to come down. Some of them tried their hand at skywriting, and some did quite well with a few letters. Finally four of them got together on their own frequency and lined up over a clear patch of blue sky and made a tic-tac-toe design in the sky and proceeded to play the game, it was a terrific site from the ground.

A B25 Does a Jet Let-Down

Two jet jockeys got in a B25 one day and decided to take it up and do a jet letdown on the x-ray beacon. Jets normally do that approach starting at 25,000 feet. These two guys had their oxygen masks on and started out climbing in a circular pattern over the southeast side of the airport about 10 o'clock in the morning. By noon they had only got the big noisy bird to 20,000 feet, it was easy going to 10,000 feet, and then it became very sluggish. They both were getting hungry, and everyone else was coming in for dinner. So they did the approach and came down a lot faster than they went up.

Some Controllers that came into the profession later on got involved in other business lines. Sometimes, to earn extra money, other times to occupy their minds or time. Some did it to have a backup job in case they lost their license due to medical or other reasons. One such guy was Mike. No one could spell his last name right and he used to get put out if you asked him if he was related to a football star that played for the Saskatchewan Roughriders. Their name sounded the same but they were spelled different. Mike was slim, dark and handsome. He was a ladies' man. Some Controllers used to say he had bedroom eyes. He had part ownership in various small enterprises around the country. One of them was a dry cleaning plant, and he was forever having trouble keeping girls on staff. One time in Winnipeg, we stopped by a supplier for Mike, had a visit and a couple of drinks. Mike played a trick on the guy. He took an unmarked bottle of ammonia out, passed it over to this other guy asked him to smell it to see if he could tell Mike what it was. He said "take a good whiff of the stuff." Well the guy took a big draw through his nostrils and it knocked him on the floor and he couldn't speak for about five minutes. He was red in the face and it was hard to tell if it was from the ammonia or if he was just flaming red mad. Mike had a weak stomach, and no one knew this until one day at work he was sitting in the tower having a sandwich. Most of the Controllers would eat their lunch in the tower just to get out of the dark radar room and enjoy the sunlight for a few minutes.

Mike had started his second sandwich and Lorne was describing a mine accident where this guy that got hurt was sitting with his scalp torn off and hanging down his face. Mike turned white got up, left the tower and honked his guts out in the bathroom just below. Mike didn't come back to finish his lunch. He would even get a queasy stomach if someone accidentally pricked their finger and blood appeared.

He was His Own Drummer

There were a lot of good Controllers who could handle any amount of traffic, not get too riled up and keep their cool. They knew that the situation wouldn't last forever, even though it may seem like an eternity at times. Bob Ward was one of these.

There were many others, but I won't try to mention them here. Bob will serve. Those who could do it know who they are and those that couldn't either got out of the business or moved on to less stressful jobs in the Department of Transport. Bob could be talking to 15 or so aircraft, some doing approach practice, some doing letdown practice and commercial traffic landing or about to depart. Sometimes there would be five or six converging from different directions on base leg and Bob would be humming quietly to himself standing with a good view of the traffic and tapping his toes on the floor with a beat of his own. He was his own drummer, a non-controller could have come up to the control tower and think that he was kind of funny, not even noticing that he was handling a large volume of traffic. His phrases were short and clear and understood by the pilots. He only said what had to be said to get the message across. On the other end of the spectrum there were Controllers who would never stop talking to let the aircraft have a word and they would be in a fit of panic. Some called it " a schmoozzle on left base", they would be talking so much that in their minds the situation was desperate, they would be standing, talking louder than normal into the mic, arms flailing and moving about the tower as if they had to go to the bathroom. When all was done and the truth came out, all he had was two aircraft and they were miles apart.

The Worst Blizzard in Our Time

One winter we had the worst blizzard in our history. The day shift was about to go home, just waiting for the relief to show up when the blizzard hit. The maintenance garage is about 300 feet from the terminal building, but was not visible. One controller that had come early had trouble getting from the parking lot to the terminal. The storm came so fast and packed such a wallop that within a few minutes, everything was shut down and the airport was "notamed" closed to traffic.

By this time, the roads were blocked and visibility was zero. The cars that were in the parking lot couldn't go anywhere because of the roads and visibility. No one could have started their cars anyway, because under the hood, the snow was packed like cement right to the ground.

One of the radio technicians, Charlie Connors, had been caught halfway toward the localizer building about a quarter-mile from the terminal building. His radio was working okay, but he couldn't tell us exactly where he was. Finally, his engine stopped because the snow smothered it. His battery finally gave out and we were trying to get some help to him. A snow blower and plow were dispatched from the garage, but they were having trouble finding their way and keeping from getting lost.

Finally they found Charlie, picked him up and put him in the warm cab of the snow blower and slowly brought him back to the garage. Some of the evening shift had phoned in to say that they couldn't get to work. Nothing was moving in the city, not even the buses. We had committed ourselves to staying on until next day when hopefully things would be better.

Arrangements had been made with the restaurant for food and we had picked a place to sleep. Everyone in the terminal building was in the same boat, so to speak. The temperature had gone from plus 10F to −30F in a short time, and the wind was up to 40 mph.

By midnight things were starting to break and we heard on the radio that the plows would be out on the roads but requested traffic to stay off the roads. About a half hour later, a bus made its way to the terminal, and we all piled on and went home. There would be no air traffic moving for some time because of the field conditions and besides, no one could get to or from the airport anyway.

That was the worst storm in my lifetime and there were a lot of people stranded and a lot died because of it. Some that had been stranded on the highways froze to death right there. It was not until the next afternoon that traffic started to move again and things started getting back to normal.

Very few Controllers made a career of Air Traffic Control. That is to say, few stayed in the active control position for the rest of their careers. Some failed their medical and were given employment in other departments; some went to a place in Ottawa they set up for those who failed their medicals. It was called ARCO (air space reservation coordination office). It still exists today, although I often wondered if they really needed the place. Others went to Management positions and as the bureaucracy grew so did the new positions and titles and Controllers to fill them. Guys who were having trouble with traffic control as a career quickly transferred to another job to get away from the stress and problems. Some stayed and haunted their fellow Controllers forever and a day.

Summary

"When you introduce a moral lesson, let it be brief "-- Horace –

There are literally hundreds of controller/pilot stories that I've missed or forgotten. There are about 2,000 Controllers across Canada and each would have as many experiences in their daily lives as I have had. I hold no grudge or animosity against anyone, and there are some who think that not enough has been said about one thing, and too much about another. These are my personal recollections, and I will stand by them. If anyone has been hurt or ashamed by any of the stories I am truly sorry but that is the way of life.

There are some subjects that have been covered very lightly, not that they may not be important, but to cover all the material that I wish to cover, that is how it had to be. Many friends and Controllers have not been mentioned by name, but I do hope that they see themselves in some of the stories. I have never regretted becoming an Air Traffic Controller. The challenge was there and I took it, the same as the Controllers before me, and those that follow.

The Tower controller, the Terminal controller, the Center controller were like three different occupations, and in my time, we were obliged to command a good knowledge of all three. With the advancement of radar and electronic techniques, most Controllers now specialize in one phase of the complex network. They must have a good knowledge of the overall air traffic control system, and then choose which area of the operation that they feel most comfortable in.

The Goose Bay Labrador experience is one of those "once-in-a-lifetime" opportunities that I wouldn't want to do again, but I wouldn't have wanted to miss it either. Now that I'm retired, Air Traffic Control is one of those things. I wouldn't want to start to do it again, but I'm glad that I did it when I did. I left the service with a clean record, unscathed by aircraft accidents or deaths of passengers caused by me or the system that I worked in. The controller has to make up his own mind, when it comes time to leave active control duties. I have seen the results of some who left it too late. I would say that, "hanging on" to reach the "magic number" is gambling with another whole future ahead of you.

Saskatoon Approach Control Tower Staff 1959

Anecdotes and Short Stories - Book 10

"There is no book so bad that something valuable may be derived from it"

—Pliny

HALABY BOOK – "Reprinted with Permission"

In the U.S., the Military ran ATC during World War II and the Controllers (PATCO) didn't come into their own until the late 1950's. As Jeeb Halaby writes in his book "Cross winds" an airman's memoirs, 1978. Hampered by inadequate equipment, official indifference, and Congressional stinginess, ATC was thousands of light-years behind other government operations of a technical nature. It took a few serious crashes to bring the system inadequacies to the attention of Congress and appropriations began to increase. Just about the time the resources became more readily available, air traffic itself suddenly started booming, and the old CAA management wasn't ready to hire and train manpower needed for handling the air travel explosion.

By the time ATC had gotten around to meeting the challenges of the 50's, the jet age was upon us, and the cycle of inadequacy began all over again. Traffic in the US kept soaring and the workload of the Controllers kept increasing due to the complex, high speed nature of the traffic. The Controllers that had been trained in the DC3 era would find themselves trying to cope with the jet world.

This was exactly what was happening in Canada, only on a smaller scale. In the 1960's, the U.S. added sixteen new Control Centres with air-conditioning, indirect lighting, great display radars with a transponder system, and even snack bars. Saskatoon, along with other terminal and control centre units was in the dark ages long after this new equipment was available and in operation in the US.

Stress in the Work Place

The asset, the FAA administrator Jeeb Halaby says of the collision between United and TWA at Staten Island in which 135 persons were killed. The blame was shared by United 60%, TWA 15%, and FAA 25%. It was a slap in the face to Controllers who were victims of the system. Halaby knew this and he said. "I didn't want our men to carry the stigma of implied guilt when they were so sure in their own mind they weren't guilty." He knew the Controllers who had been placed under psychiatric care when flights they were handling were involved in a fatal crash, even though their own actions played no part in causing the accident.

Mr. Halaby's impression of the "true role of the Controller" is dumbfounding to say the least, but upper Management are sometimes way out in left field when giving their impressions. He said "the term Controller implies authority to dictate to flights." True, there are a few Controllers who think they are God, because of the height of their workplace. But Halaby also says: "a Controller doesn't really control; he or she co-operates". A Controller has a strict set of rules to work with, and when a situation arises that is not covered in the rules, and it often does, he then is expected to use his common sense and good judgment. As far as Management is concerned, though; if he's right, it's okay, but if he doesn't work out, they throw the book at him. In all fairness to Halaby, he would rather have fought the litigation, but the aftermath of the accident was overruled by Attorney General Robert Kennedy. The millions of dollars spent on litigation could have been used to improve equipment in the ATC system. Thousands of Controllers were grateful for his stand, whether it was the right one or not, no one will really know. "End of Halaby Book"

KING AIR BOOK
The King Air Flight Check

At regular scheduled times the various nav-aid's at the airport are adjusted and flight checked with the Department aircraft. The aircraft used was generally a DC3 or a Beach 18, two slow-moving airplanes by today's standards. The department purchased a King Air and began using it for the flight checks to speed up the procedure and for the comfort. The procedure usually started out with aircraft flying a constant 10 mile circle of the center of the airport at 2,000 feet. Once this is completed the aircraft proceeds to about 25 miles out on the ILS to be checked. When the ground technicians are ready, the aircraft flies inbound on the localizer and a glide path to a point near the end of the runway where a normal overshoot would be performed. The aircraft would then proceed outbound and set up for another run, while the technicians made a few adjustments to the equipment.

While this procedure is going on, the tower controller is in radio contact with the flight check aircraft and he coordinates this flight with all the others in the control zone. As this flight check is in progress, and wind conditions permit, the controller elects to use another runway for his circuits, arrivals and departures until the flight check is finished.

The flight check aircraft had come from Winnipeg Thursday afternoon and began the flight check early Friday morning. Excellent weather conditions prevailed -- calm wind, blue sky, warm day. The flight check proceeded on schedule and was completed by 2:30 p.m. in the afternoon. The pilot completed his paperwork, then went into the ATC Chief's office and complained about a near miss at the intersection of the two runways, on one of his passes across the field. He said that the controller on duty should be reprimanded. He said "I didn't want to make a fuss about it, Roger, but I thought that I should let you know".

I was the supervisor on duty that day, so Roger called me into his office and he said. "Bonzo, the flight check pilot was just in and complained about a close call at 11 o'clock this morning, do you know who was working the control position about that time?" I thought about it for a minute, and then a cold sweat came over me as I realized that I was the controller on duty at about that time. I now worried that I had cleared the flight check aircraft across the field and forgot about him, or that I had blacked out and couldn't remember the near miss. There were two Controllers in the tower at this time. One was busy with a trainee on the ground control position taking flight plan information on the landline. They both had their heads down, checking the information on the flight plan. I had just relieved the duty controller for a coffee break. There were about four aircraft in the circuit, three aircraft waiting for departure and a couple of commercial aircraft arriving from the North and East.

The active runway was 26. The arrivals were coming in from the east, the departures taking off to the west. The flight check being done on ILS 32 would be approaching from the southeast. I left the Chief's office and we went into the technicians' room and asked to have the tape pulled. It had already been taken off and stored. I wanted to replay a portion of the record to see what I had said, because I have no recollection of talking to the flight check aircraft for the hour that I was in the control position. As so often happens, when important information is needed, it cannot be found. The tape needed for the replay was lost, nowhere to be found.

I spent all of Friday night, Saturday and Sunday worrying and fretting that I had made a mistake that almost caused two aircraft to crash, and I could not recall any of the circumstances about it. The radio technician was watching the flight-check aircraft through a theodolite at the opposite end of the runway being checked, said. "I saw it happening right in front of me and I had to turn my head away because I thought that they were going to collide". This worried me all the more as no one in the tower or any other aircraft in the air saw anything unusual.

Finally, on Monday, the missing tape was found stored in the wrong box. The technician and I replayed the tape from one half hour before I started on duty in the control position, to one half hour after I was relieved of the position. There just was no conversation between myself and the flight check pilot. We played it over and over to be sure that everything was in the proper sequence, and that there was no possibility of the tape skipping or missing some information.

The only conversation between the flight check aircraft and the other controller on duty was before the time I had taken over the position, and he said that he was proceeding to the 25 mile limit and would report when established inbound on the localizer. He normally would fly the localizer, inbound to the outer marker, and then call the tower for clearance across the field and that all important call was never made by the pilot. That particular day "Bonzo" was flying the aircraft full out, instead of reducing speed on the pass over field.

My back was turned to the approach path of the flight check aircraft. There were two aircraft downwind runway 26 about to turn base leg. My attention was directed to that part of the sky because the two in the circuit were about to conflict with the commercial aircraft arriving from the North. A Cessna 144 (push - pull aircraft) with American registration had just been cleared for takeoff on runway 26, with a left-hand departure direct to Calgary. When he was clear of the control zone I wished him a good flight and cleared him from the frequency. The Cessna had obviously not seen the King Air either and he was the one that was almost clobbered.

An eyewitness report received some days later said he saw the King Air," balls to the wall" 25 feet off the deck cross the field down runway 32, and he blended in with the background horizon. That is probably why no one saw him. So the pilot "Bonzo", flying the Department aircraft almost killed himself and others in another aircraft by his stupidity, and then blamed the controller. It was a relief to me, to know that I had not made an error. I had suffered the anguish for the weekend. It was probably the worst and longest weekend of my life. The near miss gave me nightmares for many weeks to come. Even though I knew that I was not to blame, it was hard to shake the thoughts from my mind and get on with living.

DC-9's

Air Canada: Two DC-9's merge over Saskatoon.

One hot summer evening, there were thunderheads built up across the sky from Calgary to Winnipeg, and the commercial flights were having a hard time moving along the airway from west to east and being able to stay on course. Saskatoon control was set at 25,000 feet at that time, and the control of aircraft above that altitude was done by Winnipeg Center using standard separation. A bit of politics dictated that Winnipeg handles the control above our airspace, even though radar was available (a few years later this was changed). The radar display was the one dimension. Aircraft targets would often merge, but we had no idea of their altitude.

The Winnipeg controller had called on the phone to say that due to the weather an Air Canada DC-9 en route from Calgary to Winnipeg would be detouring a bit north off course. A short while later he called again to see if we could see him on radar. Without identifying an aircraft, it was only guesswork to identify

Anecdotes and Short Stories - Book 10

an aircraft with the small amount of information that we had. The Winnipeg controller was beginning to worry about an Air Canada DC-9 enroute from Edmonton to Winnipeg at the same altitude, so he decided to change both aircraft over to our frequency so that we could identify them and keep them separated. Just as the two DC-9's reported in on the frequency, one blip came out of the overhead null in the radar heading east. On the next sweep of the radar the blip split into two blips, and we did not believe our eyes. We asked the pilot of each aircraft to identify, and both were identified and separated.

The pilot asked. "How close do you think we were?" and the Controllers said, "I don't know, both targets had merged over the airport." The secondary slash of a transponder covered about 3 miles on our radar, so they could have been anywhere from wing tip to wing tip, to 6 miles apart at the time that they crossed paths. The aircraft originally flying Calgary to Winnipeg had detoured further north than he had expected and had come through some rough weather trying to get around the wall of CB's. They were also flying in cloud so would not have the opportunity to see out the window.

Air Traffic Controllers Anecdotes

There was a controller that had become a burr under the Chief's saddle; this was not by any means the first one. But this was an exception. He was always goofing off without telling anyone where he was going. He was a great artist and could draw cartoons as good as Wicks. His controlling capabilities were fair, but he was unreliable, one never would know for sure if he was going to show up for work the next day. He was married, no children, and wife working so he didn't have to be at a certain place at a certain time as far as family life went.

He was going to get into the importing business with a company that manufactured exclusive glue for aircraft model builders. His first order came to Customs and they seized it, not to be released

Air Traffic Control   129

because the label was not in two languages. After a great argument with Customs, which he lost, he went out of business. Not to be deterred though he negotiated for the ownership of a large hobby store on 2nd Ave. everyone including his banker had advised against the deal and he backed out at the 11th hour. He took off on a trip west and told his wife that he was going east to Winnipeg. He ended up on the coast of California somewhere and a woman convinced him that he should come down there and go back to school. Within a couple of days, he made the announcement that he was going to California and become a brain surgeon. He hadn't told his wife that he handed in his resignation as an Air Traffic Controller and was going to bum a ride west the next day.

It was a Sunday morning and he was out to the airport to wait for a ride with any aircraft going west. There was a small American Cessna arriving on the ramp to drop some passengers and flight planned to Havre Montana. Jack ran out to the airplane and asked the captain if he had room for one passenger. He had to turn Jack down because it was against his company policy to carry unauthorized passengers.

Jack came back into the terminal and made the announcement that he had changed his mind, he was going to come back to controlling aircraft. He went to the Chief in the morning and made his request. The paperwork had been completed on his resignation so he was actually a non-employee. The Supervisors and the Chief of the unit had a meeting and all were in agreement that he should not be rehired.

Ottawa insisted that he be rehired because it would save them a lot of money, not having to train someone. He was rehired and sent to Toronto centre. They didn't want him so they sent him to the school to teach new Controllers how to do it. Of course, this action was not new to ATC. Several years before that when the Saskatoon Staff was going to be cut in half, one controller decided that a career in the Air Force would be good for him. He would see the world and get good pay, while he was at it. They agreed to take him into the Air Force as Flight Lieutenant Controller. He signed up on a Monday, had a farewell party on Tuesday and he cancelled the whole thing on Wednesday. He was rehired into ATC.

One of the old T-33 navigators, who was a Controller at Saskatoon got Ronnie's wife cornered in the kitchen the night of the party and told her the true facts of life about life in the Military. He told her that the Officer's Mess came first, and she would be second in his life. She didn't believe that, but as the night went on, she became convinced that she would not like what Ronnie was going to do.

As I said, Doug was a practical joker, and one Sunday morning when there was not an airplane in the sky for 100 miles the radio operator called up on the hot-line for some information. After several calls and no answer, Doug called down and said to "notam the tower closed, we're too busy". The operator took him up on it and sent the message out on the teletype lines. It took very little time for reaction from Ottawa, and they wanted to know why the tower was closed. There had never in all life of ATC been a period when an airport had been closed and this was the first, so it must've been important. Well the guys got on their bicycles and pedalled backwards as fast as they could and were able to salvage a disaster without anyone getting fired.

Jim was a handsome young fellow with jet black hair and a bushy mustache who used to work for Environment Canada before coming to ATC. Jim was a night person, that is to say he was useless in the early mornings and had a terrible time getting up in the mornings. This worked okay for Met, but punctuality was almost an obsession with ATC. If a person was expected to be at work at a certain time then he should not expect someone else to cover for him until he showed up. Jim had several citations on his record for being late, and even had a few dockages of pay. Finally someone got to him and straightened him out. He became one of the best Controllers, his whole life seemed to change and he became everyone's friend. He was another example of a controller that was about to be turfed and someone saw the good in him and saved him.

There was another controller Des, who worked not too long as a tower Controller, nor as a Centre Controller, but he had an uncanny wit of being able to talk anyone into anything. When Saskatoon's area of responsibility was 50 miles and up to 25,000 feet, by the book, we were actually doing more than was required by the agreement. This fine day there were a lot of aircraft in the sky and there were a few T-33's in holding at the Yorkton beacon at 25,000 feet under the control of Winnipeg Center, a westbound T-33 enroute from portage Manitoba to Cold Lake Alberta came up on Yorkton also at 25,000 feet. We usually got an estimate from Winnipeg on an aircraft that would be transiting our area, but we didn't have anything on this one.

We saw him on radar and saw him pass the other aircraft but thought nothing of it at the time because he probably was at another altitude. It was a clear day and the two aircraft saw each other as they passed. When the over flight came on our frequency he wanted to know why the other aircraft was at his altitude. We couldn't explain what had happened and advised him to call Winnipeg controller when he got on the ground at Cold Lake. He did just that and the line he used was a common line that we happened to monitor. Well Des got on there and talked his hind leg off and when the pilot hung up he didn't know what had hit him, and it was so convincing that he couldn't believe his ears. Something about being five minutes from the edges of the holding pattern of the other jet. Didn't make sense to anyone but if you talk long enough you wear the opponent down.

When I first came back from Goose Bay, Roger and Joel, two Controllers with entrepreneurship took me aside and tried to convince me that I should invest in their business. They had bought a soft ice cream franchise and a truck and were looking for some investment money. I was almost convinced but didn't have that much money anyway, because as soon as I bought a car there wasn't that much left. These guys worked day and night to get the thing off the ground and ran into many problems along the way. Sometimes the flavor was not right, other times the ice cream was too soft and runny. Then the truck would breakdown. They finally, after a couple of years, licked their wounds and sold the whole darn thing.

Joel was a good salesman. He went north to a resort owner and sold him a jet propelled engine for a motor boat. He convinced the guy that he would be getting in on the ground floor with these engines and they were a practical thing for him because he wouldn't even have to worry about being in trouble with a broken shear pin again. The thing used no propeller; just a force of water out the back would propel the boat. The thing was a couple hundred dollars and Joel took his money and ran, it was a good thing because if the guy had ever seen him again he would have used his shotgun on Joel. The resort owner was a sort of a shrewd operator himself and he felt really bad to be had by a city slicker. The motor was useless and sat in his boathouse to remind him of how stupid he had been. It was hard to pin the label of the "resident clown" on any particular controller, but there were plenty that qualified. One of them lived in Regina, and he streaked a shopping plaza, one day when streaking was in. He came to Saskatoon and streaked the Sheraton cavalier in the middle of the winter.

Another guy, Don Deally, we used to call him Dan Daly. He was a happy-go-lucky kind of guy and when he moved to Winnipeg tower, I always went to see Don to get his gut reaction on how he thought ATC would be going in the years to come. He used to say, "They're going to have to install turnstiles in a few years because the Controllers would be going out so fast you wouldn't be able to keep track of them". Well, he was pretty close to right because the rush started about 1980 to1981 and is still in progress. Reg Webb was another clown, who was really good at imitating people. He could imitate a Supervisor or a Chief complete with some terrific sayings, change his voice and put on a really good show. He could also drink beer and proved it one day in the pub in Winnipeg. There was a hotel called the Hangar near the International Hotel. He was promised a trophy for his feat but never did collect. We had been in Winnipeg for a week's refresher course and Reg was sick on Wednesday but showed up near the end of the day. He looked in terrible condition and should have been in bed. One of the Center Controllers saw this as a chance to make some money, so he convinced the beer drinking champ of the centre that he could beat Reg, no problem because he had been sick all day. We all went to the Hangar for a couple after school, and there was a group of about five or so from the centre, and about five or six from the school. The manager of the bar was convinced to let this thing happen.

So we set up a table with two full bottles of beer. Mike, who had instigated this whole thing, was going to be the timer and he had his watch ready, and everything was ready for the word "go". Mike said "go" and looked down to his watch to get the time but before he could look up Reg had quaffed the beer and set the empty on the table. His opponent was still guzzling and hadn't half finished. There were a few strangers in the bar to watch this and they couldn't believe what they saw. We collected our money and left. We were touting him around as the Champion beer guzzler, but his dad said. "I don't see anything so great about being able to drink beer the fastest". He was right, but Reg was so funny about the whole thing that he kept everyone in stitches. Reg was the only guy that could imitate all the characters from the Muppet show. I guess he used to spend a lot of time with his kids when they were small watching some of the children's programs, and he would get his practice there.

One of the Controllers that was just on the fringe of being "in" or "out" as a controller, used to practice war-games in his spare time. I guess there are a few who get a charge out of setting up a battlefield with so many thousand men and tanks and battleships and try to outsmart someone else, who was interested in the same kind of game, something like a game of chess only that they called it war games.

When Doug Henault came to Saskatoon he had a couple of rough years, probably because he didn't have enough outside interests to satisfy his enthusiasm. He soon got onto physical education at the local Y and had the whole airport staff jogging, exercising and more concerned with their health. Most stopped smoking. He tried to promote a workout area, shower and change room with Ottawa, but his letters had fallen on deaf ears. I hated to discourage him in his efforts, because I had tried the same thing several years before and got a cool reception to the whole idea. But a few years later, health became the prime interest of the Department and they even set up a health club in Toronto Centre for the employees. It seemed like they were saying, if you can raise the money yourself, you have our blessing, but any money spent by the Government would be spent in Eastern Canada.

Another story... not funny for all

Digging into my files again I found this little gem. Some may recognize it, some may not, and it isn't funny for everyone, so here it is.

One Sunday morning when things were quiet, and there were no Air Force flying on the weekends except the transients coming and going, one controller decided to take a walk and get some fresh air. There were just two of them on duty that day. He walked over toward the maintenance building and spotted the truck parked outside the building. It was pointing towards the tower and the keys were in it. The devil got to him and took over, and he got in the truck and revved up the engine with the windows down. He made a transmission to the tower pretending to be an aircraft about 10 miles southeast of the airport and asked for landing instructions. The noise sounded like a regular transmission from an aircraft so, the tower controller didn't suspect anything. He shut off the engine closed the truck door and walked back to the terminal building.

He waited a little longer then went up the stairs to the tower, he got briefed from the other controller and said he had the picture and would look after things. The other controller was quite worried about this airplane that had called some time ago on the ground control frequency and sounded like he may have had engine trouble. He had already called Winnipeg and alerted search and rescue so didn't want to leave the tower until he saw what the ending would be. Billy finally put on the stern look and ordered the other controller to leave and have a break and that he would look after things. As soon as the other controller left the tower, Billy phoned Winnipeg to straighten the whole mess out. There was no harm done and it had been caught before things got too far gone.

Tom was a good controller and he was very conscious about his appearance. He had to work the midnight shift, then catch an Air Force DAK on to Winnipeg right after shift in the morning. So he had come to work with his lunch and a small suitcase for his trip the next day. When the traffic died down about three in the morning, lights were turned down in the tower and the field lights turned off. Controllers were known for their adeptness for sitting in a chair and falling asleep for 40 winks when time was dragging in the wee hours of the morning. But this guy had it all, he took off his good clothes and hung them neatly upon the back of the chair and put on a pair of pajamas so that the pants wouldn't get creased. Only thing the controller coming on duty in the morning came early and caught the other Controller still in his pajamas.

There was a controller in Winnipeg, who would quite often fall asleep right at the control board. They usually work in pairs in the Center, one on radar and one coordinating on the board and the phone. Another controller would be working away and turn to ask Don for some information, but Don would have fallen asleep. So one evening Don fell asleep in his chair and when the midnight shift came in one of the Controllers went over to the door and told them to be very quiet because Don was asleep and they wanted to play a trick on him. So the midnight shift came in, got briefed and evening shift went home, except Don was still asleep. When he woke up it was two hours past his shift time and he was very angry at the others for pulling off this trick. He didn't think it was funny at all.

Goose Bay 1960 – 1962
Judo

Our Judo club grew with heaps and bounds, and the pilot from Okanagan Airways was a great help. We had a grading session with the group and with the help of the U.S. judokas were able to upgrade some to orange and green belt status with the understanding that when they get on the outside and established at another club they would prove their ability and re-grade themselves at the club.

Skiing – Surprise

My enthusiasm for downhill skiing was short lived. I had loaned the set of skis and poles and boots from the RCAF stores and was practicing on a hill just out the backyard. It was heavily covered with snow and my neighbors had convinced me to try it. So I went over to the Hill and it didn't look too bad, so went down a few times and really enjoyed. It was a short hill; about 500 yards steep at the top gradually flattening out at the bottom with a long wide area.

A couple weeks had gone by, and I was able to fit in a few ski sessions. One nice Sunday afternoon I decided to go over to the hill and see if anyone was about. As I came to the top of the hill, the neighbor and a friend were down at the bottom, and they gave me the high sign to come on down. I pushed off with great confidence and gained speed on the hill, but to my surprise, they had built a jump at the bottom and I couldn't see it from the top. Well, it was too late now to change my mind that I took the jump through the air about 50 feet landed flat on my back. It knocked the wind out of me for sure. I ended up close to where the two were standing and one of them said "How did you like it?" I tried to speak but couldn't muster up enough air to get any words out. That was the last day of my downhill skiing career. I became a cross-country skier from then on and would only watch the downhillers going at it and feel quite safe in doing what I do best.

The British Vulcan's

The British had a small base on the Goose for training their crews on the V. bombers that came over regularly on training missions. There were three famous bombers where the Victor, Valiant, and the Vulcan. The Vulcan looked like it was doing 600 knots standing still. This was the Delta Wing Aircraft that could fly above 60,000 feet at supersonic speeds. When the crew filed a flight plan to go home, it contained very little information because they flew in air space that was not occupied by any other aircraft. We only had to get them above 40,000 feet and they would clear the frequency and contact their base somewhere near Iceland.

The usual procedure for the aircraft was to come over from Mildenhall or some other base in England, carry out an air refuel over Goose Bay, fly to an American Military base and do a practice bombing run and return to Goose Bay. After one or two days they would return to home base. The refuel system was not as good as the United States and they sometimes had to land to refuel. The refuel boom was a flexible coil with a couple of stabilizers at the connecting end, but it would waver around a lot and the refuel aircraft would seem to have a difficult time getting a hook up. The United States system had a more solid extended boom and the refuelers had no trouble moving in, picking up the nozzle, refuel, and be away within a few minutes.

When the Vulcan's lay over at Goose Bay they sometimes would go up the next day and do a few circuits. Well, a few of the F102's were in the circuit at the time and they are fast but they looked as though they were standing still when the Vulcan was airborne. It could turn on a dime, go fast, go slow, and was a pleasure to watch it perform.

Every year the Military would have an air show. More static displays than air displays, but all aircraft of the British and the U.S. were there for all to see. In the large-size aircraft one of the heavy-duty carriers was the C133. The Controllers had been given a rundown on the operation peculiarities of the aircraft by a couple of their top pilots. At the briefing it was made very clear that the aircraft was critical on fuel. The aircraft was used mostly for cargo and could only carry enough fuel to get them to destination if they could step climb, 2,000 feet at a time when it was requested. If they missed a step climb anywhere along the route they would have to make a decision to return to base or compute if they step 4,000 feet, can they make it to the destination?

Another peculiarity of the aircraft was that the fuselage was long and so close to the runway; it was hard to even see the undercarriage. On the drawing board was the C-141 Star lifter soon to be online for 1963, and unknown at the time though was the C-5 galaxy, the largest winged aircraft in the world.

The Korean Crisis

When the Korean crisis was at its peak, the Americans decided to mobilize the reserves and send them over to the hotspot. So all the F86's that they could muster were organized into a convoy from Military fields in the US and would be flown across the Atlantic to the Military base's there. Goose was a refuel and pit stop for the convoy and it was amazing that such a big operation could come off so well. On the taxiways adjacent to the long north-south runway, a large facility was set up to handle food, toilets, maintenance and any other things that could possibly be thought of.

The F86's would come in groups of five and break formation, landing one behind the other in close line astern landings. I was with a group of Controllers on the day shift, and the drone of jets coming and going went on all day. The Centre was exceptionally busy because of the extra workload. Amphibious Grumman Gooses where used as beacons. They were strategically located about 50 miles apart in a line from Goose to Thule across the Atlantic to form an airway for the Sabres. These Grumman's were called "Duck-Butts".

The operation was to last 48 hours and run continuously from dawn to dusk. After work, a few of us interested in seeing the operation a little closer went over to the other side of the field. It was like a beehive. Cars, trucks, airplanes and people were all over the place. The Americans had to have their famous hot dog, and there were lots of those around. Some aircraft had mechanical problems and they would be pulled off to the side and the rest of the formation would leave without them, if they could not be repaired within a certain time limit.

So when the operation was in full swing there were airplanes coming and airplanes going with five-minute intervals between formations. We watched the proceedings for about an hour, and it was just amazing how it was running so smoothly considering all the breakdowns, a few emergencies, and a lot of personnel and equipment involved. This is all carried on, along with the regular operations that normally were carried on at the Goose.

The reward of things well done is to have it done. -Emerson-

Goose Centre

The Controllers worked on the crew shift system at Goose Bay, which meant that you worked all the shifts with the same Controllers. So there had to be some compatibility between

Controllers or they would have to be shuffled around until they found one that suited them. Some Controllers were very hard to work with and just didn't fit in with a certain group. There were a lot of hard feelings, the workplace would become tense, and some Controllers would not even speak to each other. The Chief had to keep a handle on it and move some Controllers around. There were four crew shifts and it seemed to work out that three of them got all the right Controllers with good personalities and the fourth one was a mixture of all the other personalities.

The shift that I worked on had an agreement that on the midnight shifts they would have a communal meal. Everyone would bring their specialty, and we would all eat together. One midnight shift, it had been agreed to have spaghetti and meatballs with baked potatoes, onions, desert and tea. Don McCallum was from Prince Edward Island and his specialty was meatballs in sauce. Sid Bower had brought two packets of spaghetti and everyone else brought their share. About three in the morning, someone said they were getting hungry, so we should start the meal (didn't know what to call it, but if it was normal time it would be called a supper in the West and a dinner in the East). There is a small kitchen in the American quarters that they had agreed to let us use if we cleaned the place after using it. Sid went in and found a large pot, and filled it with water and turned on the stove returned to the centre. He announced "Well, I've done my share" and said it was my turn to cook spaghetti. I picked up the two packets of spaghetti and went to the kitchen. I've never cooked spaghetti before and no one would tell me what to do, and there were no instructions on the package. So when the water was boiling, I opened the two packets and tossed them in the pot, put on the lid and went back to the Center and said, "Well, I've done my share "and sat down at the board. Someone said," Did you separate the spaghetti when you put it in the water?" I said" no", and went back to the kitchen to do just that. Some of it had already stuck to itself and could not be broken apart. I stayed with it for a few minutes and stirred it while cooking and about 10 minutes or so it looked ready. It had all fluffed up and was almost overflowing the big pot. The meatballs were put on the stove to cook, and within a few minutes, everything was ready. It was one of those best meals we had had for a long time and everyone enjoyed it. There was double the spaghetti we needed and half the remaining pot was left. Someone took it to the bathroom and flushed it down the toilet.

When the day shift came in, the Centre was all cleaned up and the kitchen had been made spotless. One of the day Controllers had to go to the washroom and do his thing. When he flushed the toilet all the water came spewing out on the floor and into the Centre and the plumber had to be called in. Of course no one mentioned about the spaghetti. But it must have swelled some more and really plugged up the plumbing system.

One of the procedures in the rule book for ATC was that the unit Chief would hold a staff meeting at least eight times a year to standardize unit operation. At units with greater than 10 Controllers, they would hold the semi annual meeting to discuss current and future programs, policy and staff suggestions. These meetings were usually planned for the afternoon so that the midnight and evening shift could take part, and as many day shifts as could be released from the boards. The Chief did most of the talking, so that he wouldn't have to field too many questions, because there was a time limit on the meeting. Consequently, not too many Controllers had a chance to blurt out some of the little things that had been bothering them for the past month.

Any problems at home? No!

Our twin boys were just one year old and on different formulas. We were triple diapering, this was before the pamper throw away of today. So our clothesline was full, of diapers and with the rain it was difficult to keep enough clean and dry. We had been feeding them this powdered KLIM, and Starlac, and it didn't seem to be satisfying them. We seemed to be forever feeding them. There are no instructions with the powdered milk and we were to find out later that it had been mixed too thin, and that was the reason for the little guys being hungry all the time. Goose was a good place to raise children because of the open spaces to play and no worry of traffic. The only vehicles were the bus a few trucks for garbage collection, and maintenance and a handful of private vehicles. All were very careful around the living quarters and always traveled about five to 10 mph, while in the area. Every Wednesday was a bus run to Happy Valley, and this was a big thrill for everyone to get off the base for a couple of hours and look through a few different stores. The bus was always full, so it was a popular event. Anyone wanting to go to the American base had to make their own arrangements. Most would try on some social gathering at the American base and babysitters were a premium, so a person had to plan well in advance to get someone. For most of the time on the Goose we had a young girl was the daughter of the airport manager. For the number of times that she baby sat for us, she never once had seen the kids. They always would sleep through till we came home. So one day before we left we called her to come down during the day so that she could see the kids she had been sitting for all this time.

Once a month stars would be brought in from stateside to entertain the troops and sometimes we could get tickets to see the show. Bob Hope was there one year just before Christmas, and everyone enjoyed the troop of comedians, on their way overseas to some of their European stations.

During the first winter we ordered a bicycle from Eaton's in Montréal and it came on the first boat in June. This was an ideal way to get around because the paths through the woods were smooth except for the odd stumps sticking up and a few branches that hung down a little low. One evening I was life guarding at the pool, so I took my bike for transportation. After the pool closed about 11 o'clock I stopped at the Squirrel Club for a beer and had a few, forgetting that I had the bike with me. When it was time to go home I had a difficult time through the woods because it was so dark and I kept on running into trees. I finally got off the bike and walked the rest of the way home.

Jim's show

One of the Controllers decided to cut his own hair because he thought that he was in the north and no one would notice. Also he could save two bucks by doing it himself. So he got out his scissors and with the aid of a mirror began to cut. It was a little choppy, so to try and smooth it off he picked up his electric shaver and began to trim a little closer. The result was outstanding (as the man on TV would say), it was a mess and he had to go to work the next day. Well, the guys at work gave him the raspberries, and he could hardly wait till the day was over. He had made an appointment with a barber on the RCAF base to try and patch up his mistake. The base barber was always busy, and to even out the flow of people waiting everyone had to make an appointment for a slot time then sit in the shop and wait anyway. Well Jim made his appointment and went straight to the barber's after work; his face was still quite red from the embarrassment of the day shift. When he went into the barber shop, the guys inside couldn't contain themselves. They started laughing and it seemed that the price of a haircut that day was well worth it. The barber laughed so hard and so long, it really made his day. He just couldn't charge Jim for the haircut. It probably was the first and last time that he had laughed so hard since he started barbering.

That of course was the last time Jim would cut his own hair. Others had tried trimming, but no one would want to be the laughing-stock on the base after seeing what Jim had to go through. There was another barber over on the American side and his haircuts were cheaper. But you must remember this was a Military base and everyone gets the same haircut. Brush cuts were still in style then but not the type that the Military like to give.

My Brother Doug

Some stories about my older brother Doug, who lost both his legs below the knees, at the age of 19 while serving in the Canadian Military in Italy. His 21st birthday present was a brand new set of artificial legs. His way to carry on a productive life without complaining made us all feel ashamed of our menial complaints from time to time.

After our wedding and reception in the old CPR railway station in Moose jaw, Jean and I boarded the "skunk "to Regina. The train was called the skunk because of its smell from burning diesel fuel. The rest of the party carried on the celebrations at the home of Jack Pye on the east side of town. April 20 was a cold and snowy day in 1951. There was about an inch of snow on the ground. Jack's house was a very small, old wood frame constructed place, bulging at the sides from the small crowd of revelers. The house soon became smoke filled and hot. Doug and a few others decided to step outside for a breath of fresh air. Because of the mud and wet, he had taken his shoes off of his wooden legs, and was just in his stocking feet. Five or six of them were standing around outside in the snow. Jack's wife, Marge called out to Doug. "Get inside here before you catch pneumonia, out there in your stocking feet."

One time after our return from Goose Bay Labrador, my brother, Doug and his family were visiting us in Saskatoon. Our twin boys were two years old now, and Dave was playing ride- a leg-horse with Doug, in the front room. Dave fell off and was starting to pull on Doug's foot. Doug had just received a new set of legs that required no harness. As Dave was pulling, Doug relaxed his muscles and the whole leg came off. Scared the heck out of Dave, and he got up, running to the kitchen, thinking he had pulled Doug's leg off for real. He of course didn't know that they were artificial. On another occasion, in the dead of winter, there were five guys including Doug out on the ice with skidoo's and fishing gear. It was a bitter cold day in Regina Beach. All the guys had on extra underwear and heavy parkas and mitts. Doug was the last to arrive at the afternoon fishing session. He jumped off the skidoo, and walked over to the others standing in a circle around the ice hole. Doug looked out of place with just a pair of black oxfords, as the others all had heavy skidoo boots on. They were stomping their feet, and one of them became very concerned. He whispered to the guy next to him that Doug should get some warmer shoes on or he'll freeze his feet. The guys never said anything, and Doug didn't say anything, so the one that was concerned blurted out that he couldn't understand how come Doug's feet were so warm, with just those flimsy shoes on, and everyone else was freezing. They finally told him about the artificial legs and they had a hearty laugh about that.

TRAINEES FROM NIGERIA AND GUYANA – Training in Saskatoon

In 1966 there were about 25 Nigerian students brought in to Canada under the NATO training system to train Air Traffic Controllers. Saskatoon got two of these and Regina got two, and Winnipeg got a few and the rest were spread all across the country. Of the two that we got, one was 6 foot 8 from the **Ibo** tribe. The other was about five feet and from the **Yoruba** tribe. Now these two guys were as different as black and white.

The Ibo's name was Dele Najamo, and he was tall, slim and black as an ace of spades. He was a very pleasant person with a deep hearty laugh, which took us about three weeks to get him to loosen up with us. He was a professional tennis player. He beat the top seeded players here in Saskatchewan, and won the singles trophy at a tournament here one Sunday afternoon. He beat the top seeded Peter Hayward from the Riverside club. After Dele's win the rules of the game were changed so that if anyone wanted to enter in competition, they were to be a resident of the city for a year.

A couple of the headlines in the local paper were "Nigerian star fulfills tennis prediction here" and "Nigerian has impressive win over Simpkins". So Dele knocked over Simpkins first then took on Hayward to win the city championship.

Bonnie Abaku was very quiet and carried a Bible in his hand everywhere he went. We didn't know for quite some time that these two guys didn't like each other, and the fact that back in Nigeria the two tribes were fighting each other. Bonnie couldn't take a joke too well, but Dele could. We used to kid him once in awhile after there had been another coupe in Africa, who his new boss was. There were several changes in their Government in the short time that he was in Saskatoon.

These two guys shook the flying public when they first started using the mics. Very few could understand their thick English accent and would ask for repeats. After they were around for about a month the pilots could decipher their language and felt comfortable with them.

Our job was not to check them out, but just give them all the training that a normal student would get, and then recommend if we thought that they would make a controller back in Nigeria. This was a pretty tall order because we had no idea what they would have to work with at home. They may have only been using flagmen at the end of the runway for all we knew.

Dele caught on fast and we could let him control traffic under supervision. Clare Fife tried to get Bonnie to look out the tower windows and find the traffic that he was talking to, so that his instructions and clearances would have some meaning. Bonnie had a set of words written on a piece of paper that would be said for take-off and landing etc. He would quote the words without looking no matter where the aircraft were. He had his Bible with him and spent more time with his head in the book. Fife finally had to take the mic away from him and would only let him listen and not transmit.

When they were working in the radar room, it was hard to tell if they were there because of the darkness of the room. So we would call out their name and when they turned their head we could see the whites of their eyes. In the close working conditions any and all smells were present, but these guys sweated profusely, Guess their sweat glands worked a little different than ours. So with the odd cigar and pipe smell and the odd flatulence expelled by some Controllers, it was hard to handle. We had no air conditioning at the time.

About this same time the tower was undergoing some renovations, and a temporary tower was set-up in the middle of the field. Now this was very small and out in the heat of the sun. One day Dele had been drinking the night before and smelled pretty rank in the small tower and the guys couldn't stand it anymore so they told Dele to go outside and lie down on the grass and enjoy. So he did just that and had a good sleep, while the other guys were also happy.

These guys were gone after about four months, and Winnipeg just didn't believe some of the stories that we had told them, and they insisted that we didn't know how to train them. They wanted them in Winnipeg for awhile to straighten them out. Well, what a surprise they got, and they had all of them for a month before they were to go to Ottawa for the rest of their training. They were smarter than most of management thought and they milked the system for everything they could get before they had to go back home.

A few months later we got a group of four from Guyana, and these guys were altogether different. They were about four foot four if that, and dressed to a tee. They were very fussy about the way that they looked, and they looked good. These guys were hard to understand also, but didn't take as long to learn as the others. They were here strictly for work and that's what they did. No time off for coffee breaks and just 30 minutes for some lunch. They came in well before their shift started and stayed after each shift. They didn't talk too much with us, and it was a long time before we found out that one of them was the leader, and he kept them in strict control. If he said do something, they had better do it or they would be sent home. If there was a question about their training, the spokesman would approach the Chief instead of any of us in between.

They were a good caliber of controller and impressed everyone with their control and conduct, a real feather in the cap for the Guyana people.

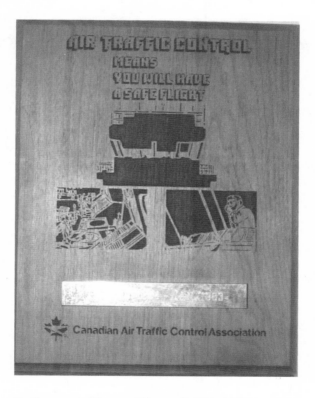

Retirement Plaque Farewell Gift 1954 – 1983

Roy Cushway and Kjell Sundin

(Two old Controllers meet again in 2013 in Penticton)

Names Of Controllers That Worked In Saskatoon, Over The Years.

A

Abaku, Bonnie
Anderson, Ron
Armour, Dave
Arnell, Bruce

B

Barnes, Ed
Bartley, Terry
Biegalke, Ron
Billingsley, Lorne
Bingham, Tom
Briand, Richard
Brown, Jack
Brown, Rod
Brownlee, Terry
Bryksa, Emil
Buchanan, Jim

C

Calhoune, Dave
Chetham, Ted
Clefstad, Duane
Cook, Al

Conway, Jim
Cousins, Roger
Coutts, Wayne
Cowan, Dick
Crouse, Jim
Cushway, Roy

D
Davidson, Marty
Davis, Paul
Dawley, Stew
Deally, Don
Decae, Ed
Derbyshire, Art
Drew, Neil

E
Epps, Jim
Evaschyen, Mike

F
Fehr, Lorne
Fernets, Terry
Fife, Clare
Findlay, Doug
Francis, Roger

H
Hamilton, Scotty
Hannah, Cliff
Hayden, Frank
Hayes, Tom
Henault, Doug
Hide, Bernie
Hodge, Brian

Howe, Rae
Hudson, Mike

J
Jakes, Richard
Johnston, Ken

K
Kautzman, Ed
Kotelmach, Ed
Kraft, Frank
Kuxhaus, George

L
Lang, Phil
Larson, Elwood
Leger, Ray
Lynch,Bob

M
McCallister,Bud
McCallum, Jim
McDonald, Fred
McEwen, Bruce
McFarlane, Ron
Mead, Gerry
Mercer, Bob
Miller, Al
Milne, Bruce
Mitchell, Dave
Mitcheluk, Ernie
Mowbray, Bob

N
Najamo, Dele

Nash, Smokey
Nelson, Joel

P
Page, Charlie
Panych, Steve
Pihlstrom, Ernie
Pischak, Ted
Pitcher, Laurie
Power, Bob
Prokopchuk, Ron

R
Read, Garry
Read, Jack
Roloff, Tom
Rooney, Terry

S
Schneider, Joe
Shura, Vic
Skinner, Vic
Smid, Dennis
Smith, G.G.
Smith, Reid
Smith, Rennie
Sneave, Orville
Steiger, Marty
Stinson, Dale
Stone, Roger
Sundin, Kjell
Surdu, Len

T
Taylor, Ken

Thornquist, Ernie
Tomecek, Elmer

U
Ulicki, Pat
Ugandan Trainees:
Augustine
Sam
Gechu

W
Wallace, Doug
Ward, Bob
Webb, Reg
Westphal, Fred

Other Than Air Traffic Controllers @ Saskatoon (YXE) Over The Years

METEOROLOGY:

Bauer, Don

Buchanan, Joe

Favelle, Ed

Hannah, Cliff

Hunter, F.G.

Pacholik, Cass

AERADIO:

Andrews, Wally

Blomquest, Jim

Dobson, Clark

Fenton, Ted

Ferniuk, Bill

Hackle, B.R.

Kauxhaus, George

Klatt, Elmer

Medlicott, L.H.

Mitchell, Frazer

Muir, Ian

Ortmann, Ray
Roney, Cliff
Schilling, Otto
Smith, Bill
Strath, Don
Webb, Reg Sr.
West, Merv

FIRE
Bates, Bob
Cummings, Len
Jennings, Bob
Kool, Blair
Milme, R.J.
Obray, Larry
Rutter, John (Chief)
Samson, Al
Sorge, Cliff
Wright, Gus

MAINTENANCE
Bordenave, Leon
Boyle, Russ
Evans, M.F.
Gamwell,G.L.
Lougheed, Harold
McMahon, Don
Petrucha, Mike
Rubbins, Robby
Ritz, R.M.
Soster, Earle,
Taylor, G.E.
Winefield, M.T.
Zakreski, Wes

AIRPORT MANAGERS

Krysowaty, M
Heasman, Eileen
Meakin, Lou

Saskatoon Approach Control 1959

*Roger Stone, * Ron Anderson, * Lorne Billingsley

Al Cook, Roy Cushway, Clare Fife, Roger Francis, Scotty Hamilton,

"T" Ed Kotelmach, * "T" Ray Legere, Fred MacDonald, Ron McFarlane,

*Bruce McEwen, * Joel Nelson, Ted Pischak , Bob Power, Marty Steiger

Kjell Sundin, * Elmer Tomecek

OTHERS WHO TRAINED AT SASKATOON – SOME STAYED, SOME LEFT, AND SOME DIED

*Reid Smith – Vic Shura –Wayne Coutts – Rae Howe – Ed Kautzman – Jim Buchanan – Doug Findlay – Bob Lynch – Al Cook – Ernie Thornequist - * Nel Drew - * Jim Conway – Bud McCallister – Terry Fenets – Dennis Smid – Rennie Smith – Smokey Nash – Mike Evashyshyn – Richard Briand – Stu Dawley – Jim Crouse – Rom Roloff – Terry Rooney – Doug Henault – Jack Read – Orville Sneave – Lorrie Pitcher – Charlie Page – Terry Brownlee – Frank Hayden – Dave Armour – Garry Reid – Bruce Amell – Jim Epps – Paul Davis – Bob Mercer – Ken Taylor – Daly Najamo (Training from Nigeria) – Bonnie Anno (Training from Nigeria) – Dick Cowan – Terry Bartley – Jack Brown - *Art Derbyshire - * Len Surdu – Reg Webb – Phyl Lang - * Ted Cheetham – Bob Mowbray – Fred Westphal – Mike Hudson - * Jim McCallum - * Steve Panych – Bryan Hodge*

*...Those are long gone to that Control Tower in the Sky

GLOSSARY

ADF — Automatic Direction Finder. Used by the controller as a nav-aid before the days of radar.

AERODOME — a defined area of land or water used or intended to be used either in whole or in part for the arrival, departure, movement, or servicing of aircraft and includes any buildings, installations, and equipment in connection therewith.

AERODOME Traffic Zone — an airspace extending upwards vertically from the surface of the earth to a specified height and designated as such in the designated airspace handbook.

AIRWAYS — similar to a road map but in the air and formed a network of routes used by all aircraft in North America. Most airways lead to or depart from an airport.

AWAYS AND AIRPORT SURVEILLANCE RADAR (AASR) — A type of radar giving directional information only. Our radar was built by Raytheon Canada and was the first installed in 1958. It is set at 180 miles distance, with two other settings available at 80 miles and 20 miles. Saskatoon was the first installation in Canada.

ALTIMETER — an instrument for measuring altitude. Three pointer altimeters, though dangerously susceptible to misreading, are still in use. Digital readout altimeters are the safest now in use. Altimeters based on radar are far more accurate than those based on barometric pressure.

APPROACH — getting the plane safely through the weather and other traffic and onto the runway. Various approaches from worst to safest are radio range, radio beacon, circling, VOR, ASR, ILS, PAR. See listing under each approach.

AIRSPEED AND MACH INDICATOR - an instrument that tells the pilot his speed through the air. Information that he will need to avoid exceeding maximum speed or stalling when attempting to land.

AIRCRAFT ACCIDENT - any accident that takes place with an aircraft from the time it starts its engines on the ramp until it shuts down at its destination.

AMIS - Air Movement Identification System - a system used to track and identify all aircraft flying in North America. Was a part of the military defense system.

ARCO - Airspace Reservation Coordination Office. Situated in Ottawa and is responsible for plotting and approving on the airspace reservations in Canada. Usually only requested from the Military for a particular exercise.

AF Air France.

ANGELS - anything that shows on the radar that cannot be determined. This could be birds, ground traffic, moving leaves on the trees, inversions.

ATC - Air Traffic Control.

BASE LEG - an aircraft on left or right leg after coming off the downwind and about to set up for final approach.

B STAND - where Air Traffic Control Assistants worked, on a small platform, behind a Controllers board. The Controllers area was designated the A-Stand.

BLIP - as the radar antenna sweeps in a clockwise direction energy is sent out on a frequency, hits a target and is reflected to the radar screen, it is returned to the radar scope and shows up as a blip on the screen.

CALPA - Canadian Air Line in Pilots Association. The commercial pilots union.

CEILING - altitude of lowest cloud deck.

CHECK RIDE - a flight on which the Ministry of Transport Inspector accompanies the pilot and grades him on his overall flying ability. The Military use their own flight check examiners.

CIRCLING APPROACH - when the center line of the runway, and the navigational approach aid to use differ by more than 30 degrees, a circle must be made to land. The pilot descends to approach minimums, sights the field, and turns his aircraft downwind. He gages his landing solely on ground clues and runway lights. A primitive approach method.

CLEARANCE - ATC clearance or instruction constitutes authority for an aircraft to proceed only in so far as known air traffic is concerned, and is based solely on the need to safely expedite and separate traffic.

CROSSWIND - opposite to base leg. When the aircraft just takes off and at the safe height turns crosswind to join downwind.

COMPULSORY REPORTING POINTS - a beacon or fix that is used by aircraft to report their position to an ATC unit and is compulsory to do so.

C/VFR - gives the pilot all the clearance copying practice and procedures of the IFR aircraft except he must maintain VFR at all times. Also used by photo mission aircraft to fly in the higher altitudes in certain areas on clear days to get aerial photo work done.

CATCA - Canadian Air Traffic Controllers Association.

CONTRAIL - a white trail in the sky behind the jet engines caused by the temperature variance between the engines condensed air and the outside air at a particular altitude, usually a moist air condition in a section of the sky. If conditions are right, the trail will stay for some time after the aircraft has passed.

CONTROL AIRSPACE - an area of defined dimensions where positive traffic control exists.

CONE OF AMBIGUITY - often referred to as the cone of silence by Controllers because that was easier to say. It was the area directly above the radar, which becomes larger with the rise in altitude in which radar targets cannot be relied on for position accuracy.

CAT - Clear Air Turbulence.

CAVU - Ceiling and Visibility Unlimited. Pronounced "KAVOO".

CADIZ	– Canadian Air Defense Identification Zone.
CHAR, CAPLIN, SCAD	- Fish points off the coast of Labrador used as reporting points for aircraft.
DISCREET FREQUENCY	- a frequency that would be used for only one special purpose. It was usually designated as such in the charts and maps.
DISTANCE MEASURING EQUIPMENT (DME)	- a navigational aid that tells the pilot his exact distance from a VOR station on the ground. (See VOR)
DEPARTMENT OF TRANSPORT (DOT)	- The Government Agency responsible for flight safety. Renamed Ministry of Transport (MOT).
DOJO	- a place where people practise Judo.
DOWNWIND	- with the wind on the downwind leg in a landing pattern called the circuit. A kind of racetrack pattern to the side of the runway.
DOPLAR	- another long-range system, not as popular as LORAN.
EAP	- exceptional in all phases. A term pinned on some pilots whose ego led them to believe that they would never err.
FIR	- Flight Information Region. An area where there is no positive control, but known flight information is given to aircraft flying in those areas.
FULL STOP	- when an aircraft lands and comes to a full stop on the runway.
GLIDE PATH	- a signal from a radio transmitter. Approximately 1,000 feet down, and to the side of the runway, which guides the plane to the runway and at an angle of 3 degrees. It is part of the ILS system.
HAND OFF	- a procedure whereby a controller would relinquish control of an aircraft to another controller at a predetermined position or point. The other controller could be in the same room, beside you, in another room, another building in another province or another city.

HYDROPLANING - the sliding that occurs when there is a thin film of water on the runway separating the tires from the surface, making breaking impossible.

ICAO - International Civil Aviation Organization.

IFATCA - International Federation Air Traffic Controllers Association.

IFR - Instrument Flight Rules.

IFR CLEARANCE - a clearance issued to aircraft flying under the instrument flight rules and includes directions to proceed with certain restrictions to a specific point.

INSTRUMENT LANDING SYSTEM - an approach system, enabling the pilot to align the aircraft with the runway by instruments. The whole system includes outer marker, middle marker, localizer, and glide slope.

IDENT - when an aircraft is positively identified by a fix marked on the radar scope or the aircraft is turned sufficiently to identify the turn. (See SQUAWK IDENT)

KLM - Dutch World Airlines.

LOCALIZER - a radio transmitter placed on the far end of the runway to give the aircraft directional guidance to the end of the runway, part of the ILS system.

LOG BOOK - a book kept at or near the working position of the controller in which he/she must sign in at the beginning of a shift and out at the end. His/her signature means he/her has read and understood everything heard that day. He/she enters any relevant happenings during his/her tour of duty.

LORAN - Long Range Navigation system used by some airlines flying the Atlantic.

LIGHT GUN - a large light with a cross haired sight on it, and a control to change the color of the light to red, green or white. This would be aimed at a nordo aircraft when on final approach and the pilot would take the necessary action.

MACH NUMBER - the speed of an aircraft as compared to the speed of sound at that altitude. Pronounced MOK and named after the Australian physicist Ernest Mach. The true airspeed had always been used by Controllers for speed calculations until the aircraft began filing flight plans using MACH number. New separation standards and procedures were adopted to account for this change.

METAL FATIGUE - structural failure in the metal part of the aircraft, often caused by high local stress concentration. Cracks in the wings or fuselage are metal fatigue.

MIDDLE MARKER - a beacon that alerts the pilot of distance from the end of the runway (part of the ILS system). A light in the cockpit flashes at 3,500 feet from the end of the runway.

MIDIZ - Mid-Canada Air Defense Identification Zone.

NATO - North Atlantic Training Organization.

NOTAM - Notice to Airmen. Notices posted on the bulletin board in an ops room or radio dispatch office with notices on conditions of other airports.

MLO - Military Liaison Officer. Was the man to coordinate all Military operations with Goose Centre, and set up the Military exercises that had been approved, also the refuel exercises.

MOT - Ministry of Transport. The new name of the Department of Transport.

OUTER MARKER - part of the ILS system. An oral and flashing light in the cockpit signals the pilot that he is 4 - 7 miles from the end of the runway, the point where he will commence to slow the aircraft and when on the glide slope begin his descent.

PRECISION APPROACH RADAR (PAR) - an accurate radar guidance system for landing. Gives the operator both altitude and directional information of the position of the aircraft on final approach. Called GCA (ground control approach) by the Military.

PROGRESS REPORT — the report the pilot gives when passing a compulsory reporting, giving his identification, altitude, time by the fix and estimate to the next reporting point.

QUICK TURNAROUND — used mostly by Trans Atlantic flights requesting quick refuel and maintenance at the destination airport.

RADAR HAND OFF — a system by which an air traffic controller relinquishes control of an aircraft to another controller when it has been identified by the receiving controller. The receiving controller could be in another city, room, building or sitting beside him. Two Controllers sitting beside each other usually use a finger hand off, where one points to the blip on the receiving controller's scope.

RADIO BEACON — a low-power low-frequency radio used for homing by aircraft. Usually placed strategically on or around an airport.

RADIO RANGE (1) — this is the beginning nav-aid for airway system and letdown systems. At most airports in the 1930's to the 1960's it consisted of four legs, which were used for guidance by the aircraft. There were four quadrants, and each would give a distinct A or N signal and if aircraft on course the two signals blend and give a solid tone.

RADIO RANGE (2) — the office that looked after the flight planning and flight following of the VFR aircraft and AMIS (Air Movement Identification System) and did the weather duties on the midnight shift. Later the name changed to flight services station.

RADIO RANGE (3) — the range was a nav-aid that gave a series of dots and dashes depending on the quadrant the aircraft was flying in. Each quadrant had a name and when the aircraft was on one of the legs he would get a steady tone, which was a meshing of the two and signals there was a cone of silence directly above the beacon to signal station passage. Radio ranges were eventually replaced by VOR'S (very high frequency Omni-directional radials).

ROGER - a term meaning that the message has been received and understood.

ROTATE - the speed at which the aircraft nose wheel lifts off the supporting surface and the aircraft becomes airborne.

RUNWAY CONDITION REPORT - the runway report taken by a maintenance truck with an accurate reading device on it. This would give the braking action that the pilot could expect when on the runway, and any other information about ice spots or snow depths in the winter.

RUNWAY VISUAL RANGE (RVR) - the number of feet a pilot could expect to see when positioned over the button (end) of the runway. Always given to departing and arriving aircraft when less than 6,000 feet or requested by the pilot.

RVR - Runway Visual Range. A measure of visibility taken from the end of the runway, giving the pilot expected forward visibility down the runway.

SAC - Strategic Air Command United States Air Force

SIMULATOR - a mock-up of an aircraft that can simulate in-flight conditions on the ground. Used by students and pilot refresher training.

STRAIGHT IN - an instrument approach carried out by the aircraft whereby he lines up for a straight in approach without first having carried out a letdown procedure. Used by tower Controllers also, to speed up VFR traffic inbound to the field.

STROBE BEACON - electronic strobe lights at the end of the runway that flash showing the pilot the threshold of runway when visibility is poor. Also on the wing tips and tail section of some aircraft.

S/VFR - Is authorized within a control zone only and is used as a crutch to get aircraft in and out of an airport when weather conditions are marginal below VFR. There are a few riders attached to the approval listed in the Air Navigation Orders. Series 5, number one. It must be requested by the pilot and approved by the controller. Quite often pilots do not request it, but Controllers offer it to them. If the pilot doesn't understand the meaning of S/VFR, he often flies into conditions that he cannot cope with.

SEPARATION STANDARDS - the minimum standards used by ATC in Canada to separate aircraft. Sometimes it is radar separation sometimes non-radar depending on the area to be controlled.

SQUAWK IDENT - the controller asks the pilot to "squawk ident" and the slash marks on the radar scope fill in. This was a much quicker way of identifying an aircraft, although it still has some Murphy's in the system, it is fairly reliable.

ST. ELMO'S FIRE - the static electricity that would form on the top surface of the wings of aluminum type aircraft when flying in highly charged particles of air masses. The blue flame like discharges would move across the tops of the wings to the rear of the wing then be released by harmless trailing discharge tales scattered along the trailing edge of the wing.

TANK HOUSE - the area referred to in a meatpacking plant, where anything that cannot be used for human consumption ends up usually, in large two wheeled metal tanks. From this they make fertilizers, cat and dog food, plant food, etc. They say everything is used in a packing plant except the squeal of a pig.

TOUCH AND GO - an aircraft making a practice landing and without stopping, pours the juice to her and takes off again and joins the circuit downwind. Usually does several of these in an hour's training.

TRANSPONDER - a black-box in the aircraft that is automatically interrogated by a ground radar station every time the antenna rotates. When the controller asks the pilot to squawk ident, the pilot presses a button and the two slashes on the radar scope fill in for positive identification.

TURBOPROP - also prop jet, an aircraft whose motion is caused by a propeller driven by a jet engine.

TWO-BITS - I didn't realize that there would be some folk who wouldn't know a Canadian slang for a 25¢ piece. Four-bits for 50¢ piece and Six-bits for 75¢.

QUICK TURNAROUND - used mostly by Trans Atlantic flights requesting quick refuel and maintenance at the destination airport.

UNDER-RUN and OVER-RUN - the area at the end of the runway before the threshold or at the overshoot area at the departure end.

UPWIND - an aircraft going in the opposite direction, and on the other side of the aircraft and runway mentioned in the down downwind.

VECTORS - a course to steer given to an aircraft, generally to an airport around whether to FIX around another aircraft, a ground obstruction, or to the final approach path for landing.

V1 - commit speed of aircraft, the speed at which take off must be continued.

V2 - minimum speed after takeoff.

VASIS - visual approach slope indicator system.

VFR - Visual Flight Rules. Non-instrument flying in good weather conditions basically 1,000 foot ceiling and 3 miles forward visibility. A clearance for an aircraft to proceed to a specified point under the visual flight rules. S/VFR and C/VFR are special categories.

VOICE RECORDER - a device that tape records the conversations in the cockpit of the airliners. Also all transmissions to and from Controllers are recorded on 24 hour tapes in a recording room in the terminal building and stored for three months before being erased.

WAKE TURBULENCE - the wind disturbance caused by the wing tips of the aircraft as they take off and land. The wake behind the Boeing 707 is the velocity of a hurricane. On calm days the turbulence can linger for as long as five minutes.

WOXOF - indefinite ceiling zero sky obscured visibility zero in fog. Pronounced wocksoff.

1000 ON TOP - a rule used mostly by the Military to fly VFR and under VFR rules when at least 1,000 feet above a layer of clouds. Sometimes referred to as VFR on top.